THE

GEEK FEMINIST

REVOLUTION

KAMERON HURLEY

A TOM DOHERTY ASSOCIATES BOOK · NEW YORK

THE GEEK FEMINIST REVOLUTION

Copyright © 2016 by Kameron Hurley

A Tor Book
Published by Tom Doherty Associates, LLC
175 Fifth Avenue
New York, NY 10010

www.tor-forge.com

Tor® is a registered trademark of Tom Doherty Associates, LLC.

The Library of Congress Cataloging-in-Publication Data is available upon request.

ISBN 978-0-7653-8623-6 (hardcover)
ISBN 978-0-7653-8624-3 (trade paperback)
ISBN 978-0-7653-8625-0 (e-book)

Our books may be purchased in bulk for promotional, educational, or business use. Please contact your local bookseller or the Macmillan Corporate and Premium Sales Department at 1-800-221-7945, extension 5442, or by e-mail at MacmillanSpecial Markets@macmillan.com.

First Edition: May 2016

Printed in the United States of America

0 9 8 7 6 5 4 3 2 1

For Joanna

CONTENTS

PART III: LET'S GET PERSONAL

PART IV: REVOLUTION

essays written specifically for this collection

THE
GEEK FEMINIST
REVOLUTION

Welcome to the Revolution

THERE'S A REVOLUTION GOING ON. WE'RE SEEING SOME OF the loudest and most violent of its battles inside a seemingly strange place: fan and creator communities of science fiction and fantasy media. These are battles fought in the comments sections of personal and professional websites, on subreddits like /r/fantasy, and, increasingly, in popular news outlets ranging from NPR to the *New York Times*. The fandoms that have arisen around science fiction and fantasy novels, games, and other media, once confined to fan-run magazines—online and off—and old LiveJournal communities and listservs, have gone mainstream. Journalists on the outside like to call this the "Age of the Geek." Inside geek circles, what geekiness is, and how it's defined, is becoming an even more hotly contested issue. Mainstream coverage of these growing pains has focused primarily on predominantly white, male geeks suffering a keen sense of nostalgia for the days when they were the assumed default audience for pulp novels and video games.

Yet women have always been geeks. They have been gamers and writers, comic book readers and passionate fans, from Conan the Barbarian to Star Trek. So why the new backlash? Because the numbers of women in these spaces have indeed grown in the last decade. Women have gone from making up 25 to 30 percent of gaming audiences just ten years ago to over 50 percent of video game players, and 40 to 50 percent of creators. Forty percent of science fiction authors are female, as are 60 percent of readers of speculative genres. Their voices, their presence, cannot be denied or explained away with talks of tokenism and exceptionalism. Women are here.

Women like me.

Human beings are, if nothing else, dedicated to upholding their narrative of the way the world is supposed to be, whether or not that world ever truly existed. If you're wondering why there's been an explosive backlash against women in geek and popular culture, this is the reason: the status quo and mainstream ideas about how the world works must be maintained by those who benefit most from it, and to do that, voices that speak of actual reality, or a different future, must be silenced.

That means me. And probably you. And a lot of the people you know. It means silencing at least half of the world.

I have been fighting this narrative for a long time, because it is not limited to popular culture. Popular culture is simply a microcosm of our wider culture, and we live in a culture that doesn't like to uplift female voices without a fight. The fight takes its toll. I am imperfect, and I am tired, and now that I'm in my midthirties I've been able to see the cycles of rage and erasure happen time and time again, and yes, it gets frustrating.

As opportunities for women in geek spaces have risen, so too has the backlash. Anita Sarkeesian's popular *Tropes vs. Women in Video Games* video education series about problematic depictions of women in video games raised nearly $160,000 on Kickstarter and simultaneously made her one of the largest targets of abuse on the internet—no small feat considering how vast the rage of the online beast can be. A single forum post by a spurned ex-boyfriend triggered an internet deluge of threats against game creator Zoe Quinn, which rapidly organized itself under the Gamergate hashtag, an online mob ostensibly about "ethics in gaming journalism" that primarily targeted women for harassment. Riding on the coattails of Gamergate came SadPuppyGate, an organized backlash against the increasing number of women and "literary" books showing up on popular science fiction and fantasy awards ballots, in particular the prestigious Hugo Awards. In 2011, 2012, and 2013, women made up nearly 40 percent of the nominees on the Hugo Awards ballot. But by aligning themselves with the Gamergate movement to stuff ballot boxes with a slate of pre-approved candidates, a small group of mostly white, male, conservative writers (calling themselves the Sad Puppies) was able to vote nearly all of their nominees onto the Hugo Award ballot for the 2014 nomination period. Due to the gaming of the vote, women nominees dropped to 20 percent of the overall total, the lowest number since 2009. The slate of nominees included nine works associated with a small press founded by a far-right extremist who doesn't believe women should have the right to vote, and another from a press called (unironically) the Patriarchy Press. The slate was summarily dismissed by the final voters, and not a single slated work except *Guardians of the Galaxy* (which was the only work likely to have made the ballot without the slate) was awarded a trophy, and every other slated work finished dead last under "No Award."

The hate campaigns don't work. The slates don't work. Yet these targeted campaigns of hate and abuse have served their purpose in another way: they have driven some women of all races, men of color, and queer, trans, and other nonbinary people away from online spaces and discouraged them from writing in speculative fiction genres.

But not all of us. *Not all of us.* Because telling someone to be quiet on the internet to avoid abuse and harassment is like telling women that the best way to avoid being raped is not to go outside, and there are many more of us who won't be silenced, because fuck that.

What the organized haters never anticipated was that their abuse would also inspire its own resistance. I was raised on stories of a grandmother who lived in Nazi-occupied France. My great-grandfather was part of the resistance. I studied resistance movements in Southern Africa as part of my master's degree. When somebody pushes back, I know how to push harder. I have a lot of perspective on what real state terror looks like, and online abuse still pales in comparison.

This vitriolic backlash inspired and continues to inspire a generation of passionate fans and creators who refuse to be silenced.

I'm one of them.

One of many.

What are we risking by speaking up? Everything, certainly. But the far riskier business is not speaking up at all. The riskier future is the one where we all fear a madman incensed by something he read online plowing a car into our house more than we fear being hit by a random bus on the street. I am sane enough to note that the odds of the latter are still greater than the odds of the former.

The truth is that much of the hate directed at us is about fear of us. As both an essayist and a science fiction and fantasy novelist, I write about and for the future. I talk about the past to remind us that what we believe has always been true—that men and women are somehow static categories, or that men in power has always been the default, or that same-sex love affairs were always taboo—has not always been thus. Who we are, how we define ourselves, how we structure our societies has been vastly mutable over time. I talk about that because if we assume the world has always been one way, then change is not only scarier ("But what will happen if we change?!"), but appears to be impossible ("It's never been done!"). The truth is change happens all the time. It's happening all around us. As I write this, the U.S. Supreme Court has recently ruled that same-sex marriage is now the law of the land. If you'd told me twenty years ago that I'd see that before I was forty, I'd have laughed.

I would tell any woman writing in online spaces today that this is one of the best times to be a geeky woman creator on the internet. Because what the small, angry groups of detractors know, and what we are all waking up to understand, is that there is a revolution going on, and *we're winning it*. The stakes are high—not just who gets to play, who gets to create, but *who gets to speak*. With comic book adaptations breaking the box office, it's these narratives from the geek universe that are fueling and influencing our wider culture. It's a revolution being fought at all levels of geekdom—from writers and creators to readers and fans.

I've been actively writing in feminist geek spaces for a decade. I have done this, and found success in it, despite online abuse, threats, and wailing for me to shut up and go home. In that decade I have become an award-winning author, one of the many building the narratives that will filter up through our culture to build the stories of the future. It has been my passion during this time to both understand and interrogate creators' responsibilities to their audiences and to the wider culture. If the stories we tell become not just books, but comic books, television series, movies, and merchandising endeavors, then what we are doing right now could have a profound impact on future generations of storytelling, which influences the behavior of our entire society. We can choose to maintain the status quo. We can choose the safe path. Or we can choose to become part of building something better.

I choose building the better future.

At its heart, this collection is a guidebook for surviving not only the online world and the big media enterprises that use it as story fodder, but sexism in the wider world. It should inspire every reader, every fan, and every creator to participate in building that better future together.

To do that requires us to become better storytellers, adept at leveling up our skills and persisting in the storytelling industry, whether that's as writers of novels, video games, film, television, or other online media.

In *The Geek Feminist Revolution*, I explore this revolution from every angle, starting with the creators who decide what stories are about, who gets to be a hero, and how to deal with backlash when we get representation wrong—or get called out for perpetuating the same tired stories. The first section of this collection, *Level Up*, includes essays about how to both improve craft and persist in the face of oftentimes overwhelming odds. The ability to persist is often a greater indicator of success in this field than raw talent.

Interrogating broken media is also key to teaching yourself how to make better stories. I've collected key pieces of media criticism and all things geek in the *Geek* section. As for the more personal essays—after all, if we can't understand ourselves and our motivations, how can we understand others?—they're in the *Let's Get Personal* section.

The final section, *Revolution*, covers exactly that. These are the pieces that poke at the wider work, and our broken systems and processes, and pull back the curtain over the "normal" society that's presented as such in media. They call for change. They call for revolution. They call for you, and everyone like you, everyone who always felt like they were out of place, like something was wrong, like the world was not built for them, to take a deeper look at what's really broken (hint: it's not you). Every geek feminist and aspiring geek feminist; every cultural revolutionary; every loud, angry, weepy, mad kid who wanted to be a hero but wasn't sure where to start; everyone who dreamed they could build something better—this section is for you.

I was once asked what my endgame was, when it came to my writing career, and the answer came easily, without a thought: "I want to change the world."

That's what *The Geek Feminist Revolution* is ultimately meant to do—inspire the people who change the world. You may not believe this right now—but that includes you, too. Your voice is powerful. Your voice has meaning. If it didn't, people wouldn't work so hard to try to silence you.

Remember that.

I understand that this is a long game, a persistence game, being part of a cultural revolution. Sometimes I need to pick myself up and dust myself off and start again, too. I am not perfect. I am not always confident. I don't always have the energy to face the day. But there are a whole lot more of us now, connected via online spaces, and all of us speaking out together are stronger than any one of us speaking out alone.

You're not alone.

Persistence isn't the end of the road, after all. Persistence is the game. The narrative that wins is the one that persists the longest, in the face of overwhelming odds.

This book is part of that narrative.

LEVEL UP

Persistence, and the Long Con of Being a Successful Writer

"PERSISTENCE."

It was the answer to a question posed to science fiction writer Kevin J. Anderson in an interview about what he thought a writer required most in order to succeed in the profession.

I read that interview when I was seventeen, hungrily scouring the shelves of the local B. Dalton bookseller for advice on how to be a writer. I'd already sold a nonfiction essay to a local paper by that point, and a short fiction piece for $5 to an early online magazine.

I felt like I was on the up-and-up. By twenty-four, I figured, I could make a living at this writing thing. By that point I'd been writing with the intent of being a writer since I was twelve, and submitting fiction to magazines for two years. Two years feels like a long time when you're seventeen.

The rejection letters were piling up. I needed some motivation.

So I wrote "Persistence" on a sticky note and pasted it to my chunky laptop.

I have it pasted above my computer monitor still.

Persistence.

The question was, how long?

I'd soon realize persistence wasn't an endgame. It was the name of the road.

When I was a younger writer, I was obsessed with figuring out whether or not I was "good." At most writing workshops I went to, from fourteen onward, I was always the best or, at least, most experienced writer in the bunch. I began writing fiction and studying fiction at twelve and sending it out for publication at fifteen. It got very frustrating. When you're in a group of people where you've got the most experience, you're less likely to learn things unless you're teaching others. And let's be real—nobody wants to learn anything from a cocky sixteen-year-old who knows how to polish a sentence.

So this yearning remained—I wanted somebody who was good, really good, way, way more experienced than me to tell me I was good. To reach out and pluck me from the fray and shake my hand and go: YOU ARE THE ONE.

It's a typical kid fantasy.

Growing up on a lot of fantasy and science fiction novels often means lying awake at night hoping that you, too, are special. That you're not just another mewling meat bag scrambling to achieve a livable wage and mortgage. Everybody thinks they could be Lessa from Pern, Alanna of Trebond, Ender Wiggin, if somebody just gave them a chance. If somebody just *noticed* them.

One of the rudest awakenings I had was when I went to Clarion West, and one of the instructors said something to the effect of, "Listen. I'm not going to coddle you all and tell you you're talented. The fact that you're at Clarion means you've achieved a certain level of good. So let's move on from that and start working toward being better."

I remember preening at this because it was the first time a professional writer ever said I was good. Thing was, so was everyone else in the class. And in every other Clarion class.

That's a whole hell of a lot of "good" writers. And that wasn't even touching on the number of "good" pro writers.

After Clarion I'd go to the bookstore and pick up books and rage because so many of them were no better or worse than anything I could write, I thought. What made them special? Why were they published and I wasn't?

My first relationship was with a blustering, panic-stricken teen who soon became a violent, delusional young man. We shacked up together soon after I turned eighteen, and shared a two-bedroom apartment. Lacking a third bedroom, the second bedroom became our shared office. He would blast endless tracks from Rush as he dithered around online while I hunched over my desk, headphones on, trying to write.

It wasn't long before my writing intensity began to wear on his self-esteem. Apparently, when he was home, and especially when we were in the same room, I needed to be paying more attention to him. I'd soon learn that this odd insistence was part of a larger pattern of seeking to cut me off from friends and family and control more and more aspects of my life—a classic abuser pattern that I wouldn't be able to name as such until I started reading feminist theory in my early twenties and found this behavior named for what it was.

All I knew at the time was that my focus on writing became a bone of contention. It elicited a lot of screaming fights and passive-aggressive behavior on his part. But as things slowly spiraled out of control in that little apartment, I found that the writing was the one thing I still owned. It helped me push through it. I might be barely scraping by as a hostess at a pizza restaurant, struggling to pay bills on time, but I could build whole worlds that I controlled totally. I could send out stories. I could survive.

But the deeper I spiraled into depression, the more all the rejection slips hurt. The more it felt like a long slog to nowhere. At my lowest point, I started to fantasize about different ways to off myself. I spent a lot of time crying in the bathroom.

And then, one day, while writing about a blasted northern landscape in one of my stories, I started to look at how much plane tickets to Alaska cost. I thought, "Well, which is crazier—booking a one-way plane ticket to Alaska or killing myself?"

My relationship eventually fell apart. I survived it, despite a lot of screaming and threats.

A year later, I booked a one-way ticket to Fairbanks, Alaska.

What folks don't realize, I think, is that very often "good" just means "competent."

I got to thinking about "talent" and the need for somebody to acknowledge it recently when I was corresponding with some younger writers. I remember how important it was to me for somebody to tell me I was good when I was slogging on the long road. There are writers far younger than me writing stuff that's far better even than what I'm writing now. And I look at these writers in their early twenties and think, Oh lord, hang on.

Because I have to tell you—being good, being talented, is the easiest part of this business. That's just when things *really get started.*

Science fiction author Samuel R. Delany once said that to succeed at writing, he had to give up everything else. He sacrificed his health, his relationships, in pursuit of becoming the best at what he did. The people who won worked harder than other people. They were willing to sacrifice more.

I didn't date for five years after breaking up with my high school boyfriend.

Maybe I was being pathological, I thought. But if I was a dude, who would question it? How many times did Hemingway shut the door and demand a room of his own?

If relationships meant giving up being a writer, fuck relationships.

When not rip-roaring drunk (and often, even then), I'd spend most nights in my dorm room at the University of Alaska in Fairbanks working on short fiction and collecting more rejection slips. My biggest win during my two years of clattering at the keyboard in college was getting accepted to the Clarion Writers' Workshop when I was twenty. This is it, I thought. In two years, for sure, I'll make it. I just need to keep at this. I can do this.

I hunkered down for the long haul. I decided I'd return to this crazy dream I had as a kid, to live in a rustic cabin in the woods in Alaska with a couple of husky dogs and just write books. I'd just write books until my fingers bled.

Clearly, I'd never pissed in an outhouse at thirty below.

After doing that a few times, I figured it was time to move on.

This business is rough on talent. Even folks who magically hit it big, monetarily, with their first effort out often drop off the face of the map within a book or two. Sure, some of this is that these folks only had one book in them. But more often, it's because the scrutiny is too much. The backend business is tough—sales, marketing, and tons of distribution issues that aren't anything you can control. And then there are the reviews and online harassment and the constant speculation from strangers.

If you get wound up too much in that, you forget all about why it was you wanted to write in the first place. Nobody is out here waiting for you, to bask in the glow of your genius. Many more are quite happy to rip you down and shit on you.

It means you have to work harder. It means you need to be eight times as good as everyone else just to stand out. It sucks. It's challenging. It can wear you down. But being good is only going to get you so far. Maybe you'll publish a few books and stories. To build a career *you need to be better than just good*. And, more importantly, you need to be hardheaded; you need to *endure*.

Durban, South Africa. Cockroaches. Humidity. Nonsensical Celsius temperatures. No air conditioning. Two bottles of wine. A pack of Peter Stuyvesant cigarettes. A master's thesis and a novel warring for my attention.

I lived in a one-and-a-half-bedroom flat with a partial view of the Indian Ocean, with nothing more than a bed and some cardboard boxes as furniture. I spent most of my time tap-tapping away in the "half bedroom," sitting on a rug on the floor, my laptop resting on a cardboard box draped with a sheet. I had books lined up all along the baseboards of the room—perfect hiding place for cockroaches.

I'd smoke cigarettes and muse that I'd finally achieved poor-writer garret-style living. But like pissing in an outhouse in Alaska at thirty below, the realities weren't as glamorous as advertised.

I submitted my first novel to publishers when I was twenty-two, mailing the proposals and chapters out from the university mail room. It was time to be famous.

Every single house rejected it.

When I lived in Chicago in my midtwenties, I'd sometimes go wander around downtown by myself. I had no real plans. No ambition. I'd just wander around this press of people and pretend my life was on the up-and-up like everybody else's seemed to be. Chicago is a big, shiny city. Like Oz blooming out of the flat Midwestern prairie.

One night I came home about ten o'clock at night after spending hours alone wandering downtown. Just . . . wandering. It was one of those aimless, "What the fuck am I doing with my life?" rambles that left me more confused than when I began.

I stumbled upstairs to my third-floor walk-up and went through the mail. In it was a self-addressed stamped envelope: me, mailing a letter to myself. You'd include them with paper submissions, back in the day when hardly anybody took e-subs, so the editor could send you your acceptance or rejection without paying for postage.

I'd put the name of the magazine I'd submitted my story to on the back of the letter. It was one of the biggest magazines in the field at the time.

I opened the letter with that gloriously giddy half-hope, half-dread feeling building in the pit of my stomach.

It was a form rejection letter. The fourth or sixth or eighth or tenth or . . . however many, that month. I could barely keep track. All the stories, and all the rejections, just bled into each other.

I had no idea what I was doing with my life, except this. I knew I wanted this. Even if "this" was just some big magazine to say yes to something.

But "this" was just one long road of rejection and disappointment.

It's strange, but I don't remember the name of the actual magazine, because it has since closed up shop.

But I remember sitting on the kitchen floor, despondent, the rejection slip clutched in my hand.

* * *

At twenty-six, I woke up in the ICU after two days in a coma and was diagnosed with a chronic illness. I received a bunch of rejections from agents for a new book not long after. One of them expressed outrage that I'd be so bold as to compare the book I was shopping to the work of Robert Jordan or George R. R. Martin, even though the query book I'd read said to compare your work to other marketable work. I filed away the rejections and wondered if I'd ever sell a book. Maybe I was crazy. Maybe I'd given up everything for nothing.

I lost my job at the Chicago architectural and engineering firm I worked for a few months later. And a few months after that, my relationship with my best friend, former girlfriend, and roommate imploded.

I found myself packing up everything I owned into the back of a rental truck with a couple of generous friends and driving my life to Dayton, Ohio.

It felt like I'd failed at everything. Life was a ruin.

I found myself living in a spare bedroom at a friend's house, unemployed, deep in medical debt, and staring at yet another novel, three-quarters of the way finished.

When I opened my laptop, the sticky note still stared back at me: PERSISTENCE.

In all things. In writing. In life.

I finished the book.

I'd reached a point in my life where I didn't know how to do anything else but finish the fucking book.

I got my first book deal when I was twenty-eight.

It came at a time when I'd hit rock bottom, professionally, financially, emotionally. It came just when I needed it. It wasn't a million dollars. It was $10,000 a book, for three books. It was enough money for me to pay off three of my four credit cards and move out of my friend's spare room.

Even when the contract was eventually cancelled, and the book never published at that house, I was still paid for the books. I still walked with the money. Thirty thousand dollars for work I never did, for work that they wouldn't publish.

I thought about all that work. About those screaming fights in that shared office with my ex, and the cold, drunk nights in Alaska, and shaking out my bug-infested sheets in South Africa, and thought, Was this it? Was this what it was about?

That money saved my life. But when the bills were paid and my life was in order again, I asked myself what I was writing for besides money, because after writing with the intent of being a writer for fifteen years, now that I wasn't dying in poverty, the money alone wasn't satisfying. It wasn't enough. It wasn't why I was writing.

Which made me wonder what the fuck I was doing, then.

Another book deal, this time a keeper, a year after my former deal imploded. Books on shelves. Elation. Joy. End of a long road, right?

No. Just beginning.

Arguments with my publisher over whitewashed book covers. Late checks. Money that stops flowing. Then the publisher implodes, sells off its assets—including me and my books.

Take it or leave it. Fight the bullshit. Rage.

Sheer, unadulterated rage, that the work I spent a lifetime to see in print is now an "asset," a "property," a casualty of shitty business practices.

I fight the situation. I persist.

I sign a new contract.

The spice flows again.

But I've lost my joy for fiction.

I'm at the bar at a science fiction convention. I made $7,000 in fiction income the year before. I'm ordering an overpriced drink that I'll be writing off as a business expense, because I'll likely lose 30 percent of that $7,000 to taxes in a few months.

While I wait, I overhear a successful self-published author talking to a group of folks about how self-publishing can make everyone big money, and how traditional publishing is fucked. I've heard this a thousand times. Kickstarter is the key, he says. You can pre-fund all that work ahead of time, and generate income. He boasts about how he gave this advice to many underadvanced authors, folks paid "these seven-thousand, ten-thousand-dollar advances," who were obviously small, silly fish. He sounds like a self-help guru. He makes writing books sound like a get-rich-quick scheme.

I take my drink. I don't pour it on his head.

I remember this is a long game. I remember that both self-published authors and trad-published authors have the same small handful of breakouts and the same massive, slushy mire of "everyone else" clamoring for signal on the long tail.

I think I've been on the long tail a long time, but the more I talk to other writers the more I realize that that whole slog—the shitty apartment with the shitty boyfriend, the frigid outhouses in Alaska, the cockroach wrangling in South Africa—wasn't actually the start of it. That wasn't the part where things got really interesting.

It was getting the first book. It was after the first book. It was being confronted with the fact that writing is a business, and expectations are very often crushed, and your chances for breaking out are pretty grim.

It's persisting in the game *after* you know what it's really all about. After the shine wears off. It's persisting after all your hopes and aspirations bang headfirst into reality.

That's when it starts. The rest of your life was just a warm-up. Anyone who tells you differently is selling something.

Last night I rolled in from a convention in Detroit at 6:00 p.m. and stayed up until 1:00 a.m. catching up on business emails and preparing blog posts. I still have a day job. I also do a lot of free-lance copywriting. Putting all that income together, I'm making close to $90,000 a year. But I've only been at that number for two years. Six months ago, half my department was laid off at the day job. I expect the hammer to come down at any time.

I expect that sometime soon, everything will burn down, and I'll have to start over.

I'm working on another trilogy. Two of them, actually. I try not to squint too much at my prior sales numbers. It might affect my game.

I'm working all the time.

In my first novel, *God's War*, my protagonist has a final show-down with the book's antagonist, who tells her, "There are no happy endings, Nyxnissa." And Nyx says, "I know. Life keeps going."

I know.

I'm packing up my stuff after a panel where I've spoken about all sorts of things to other writers, aspiring writers, and fans alike. I'm feeling drained and exhausted. An audience member comes up to me and thanks me for talking about my day job. "You just seem so successful," he says, "you've got multiple books published and you go to cons."

Later, somebody at the bar tells me it seems that every time he clicked on a link these days it linked back to one of my blog posts.

I don't feel successful.

But it got me thinking again—what's my measure of success? Is it money? Copies sold? Or is it the act of persistence itself, the act of continuing to write when everybody tells you it's a bad deal, and you should just suck it up and stop?

Persistence, I realized, was not the end goal. It was the actual game.

I had all the chances in the world to quit this game. Any rational person probably would have. Poverty, unemployment, crazy relationships, chronic illness, an imploding publisher . . . I could have quit. I could have said, "Fuck this noise."

But after raging around on the internet or drinking a bottle of wine or taking a long bike ride, I came back to the keyboard. Always. I always came back.

Most people don't.

I don't blame them.

So when people ask me now—at panels, online, at the bar— "What does it take to be a successful writer?" I know the answer, now. Now, more than ever, because I know what it actually means. I know it's not just a word. It's a way of life.

I know what success looks like.

"Persistence," I say.

And take another drink.

I'll Make the Pancakes:
On Opting In—and Out—
of the Writing Game

WELCOME TO LIVING LOUDLY IN PUBLIC SPACES — ONLINE, in print, even on billboards, if you're lucky. Welcome to being a woman with opinions navigating the court of public opinion. For my part, I've been loudly asserting my opinion on the internet and in print for fifteen years, and it never gets any better when the battle trolls ooze up from the bubbling cesspit of the internet and threaten death and sexual assault. No, it never gets easier, but at a certain point, for me, it became easier to endure.

I realized I wasn't out here on my own. I was part of something much bigger, and much more important, than myself.

There will always be trolls—the people telling you to kill yourself, the folks saying they'll come to your house and rape you in the same breath that they tell you you're too disgusting for anyone to want to fuck. They will demand your sources and copious evidence to back up your expertise. There will be men, yes, endless reams of men, who assume you write genres you don't, as if vampires and werewolves make up the sum total of women's writing; fewer opportunities for you, as a woman, for reviews; colleagues on panels who start conversations with "I don't want to be sexist but . . .", and covers for your gritty science fiction book that come out looking like a Tampax ad. Those things are going to be there for some time, to some extent. And every few years, you'll fight for respectability and a voice from a new generation of folks who don't know your work or credentials and thus judge you exclusively on gender and appearance as determined by whatever the media machine says you are. And you'll have to prove yourself all over again.

It sucks. It's hard. If you stay in the game, though, I promise you'll get very good at it. You'll get pretty good at writing, too. And business. Those are the parts that get better. You get tougher, and more jaded, and angrier as you become a better, more vocal, and more respected writer.

But you'll also get pretty tired.

I don't judge women who leave this game. I knew a lot of feminist bloggers from the early days of blogging who closed up shop after wave after wave of abuse, stalkers, threats, and real-life incidents where "internet threat" became "in-your-fucking-face threat." I know women who wrote hard SF or epic fantasy who threw in the towel, or went to genres like urban fantasy or romance that were far more welcoming to women authors. I know women who shrugged and just went through buckets of male and gender-neutral pseudonyms, and then snickered at everyone behind their hands.

So I'm not going to tell you to stay in this game.

Instead, I'm going to tell you I know it's hard.

And I'm going to tell you why, despite that bullshit, I'm still here.

I was at WisCon, a big feminist SF convention, in May 2006 when Joanna Russ did what I believe was her last public interview. Russ was in ill health, so she did the interview over the phone with Samuel R. Delany. By this time, Russ was one of my heroes. I found her to be the most angry and vehement of the feminist SF writers I'd read; compared to Russ, Le Guin was boringly conservative.

Russ expressed the white-hot rage I felt at realizing the game was rigged against me from the start, and that no matter how equal I believed I was, the world was going to treat me like a woman, whether I liked it or not. Her book *The Female Man* is so ragingly, teeth-gnashingly nuts that I couldn't get through it the first couple of times I tried. The title also gave voice to something I felt all the time—that I was a human, a man—not in the sense that I felt disassociated from my female body, but in the sense that I, too, had bought that women were somehow "other" and I wasn't "other" so I must be a man, a real human too, right? I'd internalized an astonishing amount of misogyny growing up that I didn't even recognize until my early twenties.

I bought a lot of divide-and-conquer politics when I was younger, putting women into camps: Here are the butch, strong women. Here are the weak, feminine, useless women, the kind they showed on TV as always needing rescuing. I was never Willie; I was always Indiana Jones. I strove to be part of the "human" camp of women: the strong, butch ones. But because my body was coded female, I was never, ever assumed to have the kind of knowledge or credibility that a man would have. To those who didn't know me, no matter how much I butched up, or tried to "prove" my geek credentials or masculine sensibilities, I was always just a woman on first blush. I got passed up for raises. I got relegated to admin jobs. I got money offers less than that of male colleagues.

What I learned was that I had to work harder than the guys. I had to assume that when people looked at me, they'd automatically give me crappier offers. They'd assume I was stupider than

I was. They'd pay attention to me less. They'd judge me by gender, by looks, by weight before anything else. I automatically started every interaction at a disadvantage.

In some ways, realizing this made things easier. I no longer worked on the assumption of equality. I always assumed I was starting ten steps behind. I learned I had to fight harder, shout louder, and demand more just to get five extra steps ahead, so I wasn't starting *quite* so behind in the eyes of those who passed judgment on me, from bosses to colleagues to new friends. Even in my writing career, people made certain assumptions. I remember being asked at a baby shower once if I wrote children's books. I found it difficult to even respond to that, because I'd just published a science-fantasy noir book about a bisexual bounty hunter who lops off people's heads for a living. There is of course nothing wrong with writing children's books, but I couldn't help wondering what that person would assume I wrote if I presented as a dude.

For a while I became smitten with the idea of "power feminism" or the popular "lean in" culture that passes for mainstream white feminism right now. We just needed to be smarter, faster, better. We needed to ask for raises, demand better treatment. Sexism was our fault, for buying into the misogyny ourselves, and operating like we were at a disadvantage.

But what much of that "lean in" culture doesn't acknowledge is that we do, in fact, operate at a disadvantage heaped on us by the assumptions of people in power, and thus some are able to "lean in" more than others. If I'm working a retail job and demand $10.50 an hour instead of $10, in most cases they'll be happy enough to let me go and replace me with some other hard-up person for $10 an hour. No contest. That's the game. That's how it's rigged. And this doesn't even touch on how someone will react to this assertion if you're also a person of color, or gay, or trans, or an immigrant, or acting "too uppity" for how they believe someone of your "kind" should behave. In some cases, "acting uppity" will be met not with mere job loss or scowling, but violence.

You can fight all you want for individual wins, and fight to be the "exceptional" woman, but so long as there's institutionalized oppression, bias, and unregulated, out-of-control capitalism that treats people as disposable objects, you're an exception, not a rule. So long as the people with the power—to hire and fire you, approve or deny your loan, or write up your speeding ticket—look at you through the lens of institutionalized racism, sexism, homophobia, or any other -ism they've learned from stories, videos, media, and other biased individuals, a single win means nothing.

We cannot effect true change alone.

Every writer is an island.

Often, we get tangled up in thinking our experiences are somehow singular, that no one before us walked this road or tackled these problems or felt this kind of angry woe at the state of their chosen profession as a writer of fiction, or anything else. One of the things reading Russ gave me was a sense that I wasn't on my own. When I read *The Female Man* or *On Strike Against God*, I saw myself as part of something far bigger than myself. I wasn't the only person angry. I wasn't the only person who faced bullshit assumptions about who I was, what I wanted, what I wrote. And I wasn't the only one often confused by society's expectations versus what I actually wanted.

The more women writers I read, from Margaret Atwood and Octavia Butler to Charlotte Perkins Gilman and Toni Morrison, the less alone I felt, and the more I began to see myself as part of something more.

It wasn't about one woman toiling against the universe. It was about all of us moving together, crying out into some black, inhospitable place that we would not be quiet, we would not go silently, we would not stop speaking, we would not give in.

Joanna Russ died in 2011, the year my first book, *God's War*, came out.

I remember sitting and staring at the computer and thinking, "Oh God, now what?" because it hadn't sunk in yet—oh, I could certainly admit and process the news of her death, but I didn't know what it *meant* yet. Russ hadn't really published much work since the late '90s, due to illness and, I suspect, exhaustion at this bullshit game. It's hard. It's brutal. It's no fun.

But even though she hadn't been in the game for a while, there was some safety and security in knowing she was still alive. That her voice was there. It existed. Her work was available. She wasn't going to be shut up.

With her voice there, I realized, I didn't feel as much pressure to step up.

She was there to do it.

I didn't have to.

But in that moment, I looked at my book on the shelf, which hadn't moved many copies yet, or won any awards. It was just my little niche feminist SF book. I expected it would sell three thousand copies and disappear.

That did not happen.

But I didn't know that at the time.

All I knew was that there was no more Joanna Russ, and I was going to have to find another angry, truth-telling, no-bullshit voice that I could count on to rage at the world.

It's easy to pass this buck, when it occurs to you. It's easy to point to other writers and say, "Hey, you should do/be that voice" or "Hey, why don't you take up this mantle?" or "You should really . . ." or "Writers X, Y, and Z already have this covered," but the fact is that this is a hard gig, and a lot of people drop out of it, and you never know how long they'll stick around.

I realized I could continue passing the buck, and just point to other writers speaking truth to power, because there were indeed a lot of them.

But there was another option.

Instead of just telling other people to step up . . . Well . . . *I* could be the one to step up. *I* could be one of those voices.

Because, shit: I've been screaming on the internet for ten years. What's forty more?

I don't have a lot of spoons[1] for handling this bullshit game, some days. I've got a chronic illness. I have a day job. I have book deadlines and marketing calendars and convention appearances. But one thing Russ's death taught me is that you can't rely on other folks' voices always being there. Sometimes it needs to be your voice. Sometimes, if no one else will speak truth to power, or risk speaking out against Big Dude Author X, or say "Fuck my career," then it has to be you.

There are some days where I indeed feel like I'm screaming alone on an island, the way a lot of young women writers might feel every time they read the latest bullshit about how they'll be reviewed less, stocked less, and passed over for more awards than their dude colleagues.

But the fact is I'm not alone. And they're not either. There's a huge, angry, passionate group of people who aren't happy with the status quo, and who actively speak out against it, over three hundred of whom I follow on Twitter alone. There are massive communities of feminist writers, and no-bullshit writers, women and men and everybody along and outside that continuum, who are speaking out.

They are also a lot easier to find today than they were twenty years ago, because there's Twitter and Tumblr and YouTube and easy blogging platforms. Access to venues where we can be heard is easier. It no longer feels like it's just me lying in bed with a Joanna Russ book, trying to pretend I'm not alone and writing angrily in a notebook. It's me engaged in active dialogue with like-minded folks—even if we're often arguing with each other on Twitter, and calling out each other's shit arguments and blind spots and bullshit.

And just as I take comfort in their voices, sometimes, I realize, it's my voice that needs to be the comforting one, too. When I can afford the risk, it's my responsibility to step up. Because if enough people pass the buck, and pretend this is somebody else's problem, then suddenly it becomes no one's problem, and we slide backward, and we go back those ten steps, and we go back to square one.

Sometimes they take the risk; sometimes I do. We do it together. We support each other. We argue with each other. What's important is that we realize we're not in this alone.

That's why I'm still in this game. Because I understand that much of the internet trolling, the shit-flinging, the active and passive acts of oppression are about pushing me and people like me out. It's about creating a sandbox narrative that doesn't include me or people like me. And I call bullshit.

I can't guarantee you, young women writers, that things are going to get better. I'm not going to pretend you won't get trolled, harassed, threatened, or stalked.

But what I can promise you is that you aren't in this fight alone. You are not speaking out alone, and you and your work and your voice and your passion exist on a long continuum of voices just like yours, who had to fight the same battles you fight, and who are still here, and still in this.

Just like you.

I don't blame you if it's too much. I don't judge you for telling this genre or any other to fuck itself. But if you stay in this, next to me, and next to all the other women and men and all the fabulous plethora of otherwise-identified folks engaged in rewriting the narrative of what science fiction is, we'll support you, and champion you, and we'll fight with you.

That's what I have for you. Some days, it won't be enough. Some days, it'll be all that gets you up off the floor. So you pack the guns. I'll make us some pancakes. And let's get back to work.

What Marketing and Advertising Taught Me About the Value of Failure

WORKING AT A MARKETING AGENCY IS LIKE BEING A therapist. People come to you because they know something's wrong, and they want to fix it. They barrel into your office talking about how they need something from you—they just need a flyer, or a radio ad, or a new logo. Some client relationships never get past that. At an agency I worked for, we once had a client who directed us to do round after round of endless work on a new logo, racking up thousands of dollars in billed hours, only to put the logos in front of his employees for popular vote and find that most of them preferred the old logo. They didn't understand why he wanted to change it. When he sat down and thought about it, he wasn't sure either.

Clients come to you because sales are down, or a new competitor is in town, or they've been told they need "a website" or "a radio ad." And a lot of the time you have to just be an order taker and do those things, even knowing that's not the real problem. It's like coming to your therapist and saying you have depression but what you really need to get better is a Snickers bar so if the therapist could just give you one, that'd be great, and you go on your merry way and wonder, three months later, why you're still so depressed even though you got the Snickers bar you asked for, so you say it's because you have a shitty therapist.

I have a deep and abiding love of advertising because I recognize its potential to change human behavior. Thus far it's largely been leverage to sell us all widgets, but it's advertising campaigns that reduced drunk driving, helped eliminate the pervasiveness of smoking (after getting us to smoke in the first place), and got us all to wear seat belts. I find what motivates us as human beings to be intensely interesting. What got people to stop smoking, they found, was not the ads that told you it was horrible for you—it was the ads that said it was horrible for your children. I still remember when my dad started smoking outside the house for just this reason (which led to the first of three attempts at quitting; the third time stuck). The message about "secondhand smoke" drove more people to quit or reduce their use of cigarettes than any other message. But it took marketers doing a lot of diligent studies and focus groups and, admittedly, running a lot of shitty ads that didn't work to figure out how to break the spell of "cool" that they'd given smoking in the first place.

And that leads to another one of the fun challenges of what I do: you aren't going to get it right the first time, but that doesn't mean that your efforts were failures.

I worked in-house at a large software company that did a tremendous amount of email marketing. We did so much email marketing that our opt-outs were becoming a problem. Worse, only about 50 percent of the campaigns we created were getting any responses at all. Not 50 percent of the emails that went out, but 50 percent of the campaigns. That means that we could send out ten emails to forty thousand people and only five of those emails received any response at all; even then, the number of responses was often in the single digits. As a marketing organization whose success was measured in leads we could pass off to sales for follow-up, this was atrocious. We might as well have just been flipping a coin. But instead of getting depressed by these statistics, I found myself invigorated by them. I studied the communications that had gone out to different markets. I tweaked subject lines. I made them more customer-focused. I unearthed real pain points that drove customers to make purchasing decisions. I took one particularly difficult market—sales professionals (salespeople sell things; they can smell you coming a mile away) and made a simple change. Instead of using a value proposition like "Product X helps you get organized," I repositioned it as "Product X helps you get better organized." It's not "Product X makes you a superstar." It's "We know you're a superstar. And with Product X, you'll become a megastar." Flattery works across many markets, but it works especially well with salespeople. It took sending out a flat-out failure of an email and two so-so emails to finally crack this market. I had to test and roll, test and roll with the team before we got it right, but when we did, it was deeply satisfying.

Marketing uses people's deepest fears and desires to motivate them to take actions. What those actions are is entirely up to the people paying the marketers, and yes, a lot of marketing is done badly. But the reason people keep paying for marketing is because those who do it well do it very, very well, and it took an extraordinary amount of failure to do it. It's why the folks at the Wieden+Kennedy agency have a huge "Fail Again. Fail Better." sign made of pushpins on their wall. Our job as marketers is to fail a lot in order to get to the big success. I'd like to tell you that that 50-percent failure rate was because we were pushing the envelope and learning from our mistakes, but, well, in that particular case we were doing a lot of panic marketing. Failure is only useful if you're learning from it. Failure because you panicked and sent shit out the door is just failure.

And that's the greatest lesson I transferred over from marketing to writing. If I'm going to write a book that's a commercial failure, it needs to fail in a way that moves me forward. If I'm failing at writing YA vampire fiction, then I didn't learn much except that I'm no Stephenie Meyer. I could have learned that without investing ninety thousand words in it. If I'm going to manufacture a failure, I want it to fail better. It's how I approached the writing of my first epic fantasy saga, starting with a book called *The Mirror Empire*. Like all of my books, it's a mess, but it's a mess in a very specific way. I set out to create a fantasy world no one had seen before, with societies no one had ever heard of, and I wanted the villain to be nothing less than the protagonists themselves. That's a tall order for any book. But will it be loved the way that a Stephenie Meyer book is loved? Probably not. That was not its purpose.

I don't always write a book with the intent of being loved.

I don't create marketing campaigns to be loved.

I create work to move and to inspire, and half of my job in doing that is to fail at it and learn from it and fail again even better next time. Unlike novels, marketing communications like emails and web pages and direct mailings can be written rather quickly, so I know that this process of fail again, fail better can work, ultimately. The trouble is that publishing doesn't give you twelve failures to fuel a success. Publishing gives you one shot, maybe two, and then it's back to the self-publishing mines or Kickstarter to prove your worth. Which I am okay with doing, but really?

Publishing is a broken beast, still churning along with the same payment schedules and margins and advances it had, what, a hundred years ago? I run into the same issue at large companies that insist that marketing has always been done this way, that we've always sent out direct marketing pieces and why do we have to change even though the people who buy our products have totally revolutionized the way they purchase goods?

Two big beasts. Titanics who may not have enough time to turn around.

We have to meet our consumer. We must go where they are. We have to adapt or die, and adaption requires an incredible number of failures before it hits upon the winning combination that allows an organism to thrive in a new environment.

Evolution requires change. If we don't adapt, we sink, we die, we're a panda sitting alone at the edge of a dying bamboo forest with nothing else to eat.

Some of us will change. And some won't. Maybe because, like the panda, we can't. This is all we can and will ever know. But for the rest of us, those not afraid to fail, and fail harder, and fail better: we may still have a future.

It's a future we will control. A future we will write. But we must not be afraid of it.

Taking Responsibility for Writing Problematic Stories

TAKING RESPONSIBILITY FOR THE WORDS I PUT ONTO THE page was a lesson I learned early. I wrote a short story the second week of the Clarion West Writers' Workshop, an intensive, six-week "boot camp" that was very good at wringing writers out and disassembling their prose so its weakest parts were revealed. The opening scene of my story featured a dying, tortured, and abused boy covered in blood and semen. As a mercy, since they are weeks away from help in the middle of a roiling desert, his commanding officer cuts open his throat and leaves him there to die.

For numerous reasons, the writing instructor that week took issue with this story. He said he believed it suffered from a failure of the imagination, and that I needed to be aware of what I was willing to serve up for public consumption. "As writers," he said, "we need to take responsibility for the images we put on the page."

My reaction to this critique was to go through the story and cut out every offensive part. I eviscerated the story, leaving it merely a shell of its former self. One of my colleagues likened it to chopping off all the rough edges on a marbled geode and smoothing it into a shiny faceless sphere. What I should have done instead was turn the thorny bits into proper hooks, and solder on a few more points while smoothing out the ugly bumps. Instead, I gutted the story the same way I'd gutted the characters, and created a story that was not only not offensive, but also evoked no feeling of resonance whatsoever in anyone.

If I was going to write a problematic story, I needed to either fix it or take responsibility for it.

I spend a lot of time at speaking appearances talking about the responsibilities of being a writer, and how what we put on the page can mean something very personal to people. I spend a stupid amount of time buried in research books and Googling shit on the internet and digging up first-person accounts of things and evaluating my own biases, and you know, that shit can get exhausting sometimes. Sometimes you lose focus. Sometimes you forget what you're doing it all for.

And sometimes, just like everybody else, I screw up. I write a problematic story that I can't fix.

After one of my panels at the World Science Fiction Convention in Chicago in 2012, a reader came up to me to say that she had chosen my novel *God's War* as one of her book club's selections. It turned out, she said, her book club had a number of gay men in it, and several of them were pretty pissed off when one of my major characters (and the book's only gay male character) dies about three-quarters of the way through the book.

Because, of course, the gay guy always dies.[1]

I was aware of this particular problematic trope about three-quarters of the way through writing the book. A dearth of gay characters in mainstream fiction often led even well-meaning folks to make secondary characters gay, and then kill them off without considering the long tradition of purposefully killing off gay characters in fiction simply because they were gay. Showing a tragic end for a gay character served to uphold the perceived social order in Western culture: if you were going to be gay, it would end tragically. Better conform.

Once I realized what I'd done, I picked up and rearranged all of my characters to try to rewrite my way out of the problem without killing the story. I'd already finished the first draft by that point, and I couldn't find a way to write myself out of it without completely retooling another character or adding in somebody else. I knew it was a cliché that the gay guy friend always dies. So if I couldn't eliminate the death, I could at least improve representation of gay male characters (I already had lesbian and bisexual women in the book in spades, but this particular trope still stood). I wrote a scene in which he and his boyfriend meet up and discuss what's next for them now that he has to go into hiding because he and his team are being pursued by the country's bel dame enforcers. I tried to find other mentions of male homosexuality in the world. Because I'd gotten rid of so many male characters by sending them off to war as part of the conceit of the book, I felt as though if I tried to shoehorn in anybody else it would feel forced.

And though I stood there talking to the reader about all the things I'd tried to do both here and in later books to mitigate that problematic death, the gay guy still dies. I still played into the stereotype. And that stereotype still hurts people.

I would love to be one of those writers who just says, "Hey, it's a brutal world! Everyone is mangled and killed equally!" but that isn't really true. It's like somebody saying that the reason all the female characters in their fantasy book are passive, raped damsels who exist to be saved by the hero is because it's "realistic."

Like, what? Realistic in what world? And did you forget you were writing fantasy?

Sometimes book stuff happens because that's why the book

happens. Sometimes it so happens the character who has to die is a gay guy. The problem is when he's the only gay guy in the book. The problem is when you read a lot of books and the only gay guy in the book is the one who dies in every book.

I understand that my work—and every other writer's work—isn't read in a vacuum. We have to interrogate what we're doing and understand how it'll be read in the wider context of things. And as much of a gut punch as it was for me to be reminded that seeing yet another gay male character thrown under the bus in service to someone else's story hurt people, it doesn't hurt me as much as the person who actually read it for the third, fourth, fifth time and threw it across the room because, goddammit, why the fuck does the gay guy always die?

When I challenge both myself and other writers to interrogate stereotypes, and work hard to understand how their work might be read in the context of other things—this is the reason. Because what we do has the ability to inspire and delight—or hurt and frustrate. Sometimes in equal measure.

I fail a lot at this, as this example shows. I get caught up in the bullshit just like anybody else. There's no excuse for it, and all I can do is endeavor to do better next time, and ensure that any time I do employ a trope, I'm acutely conscious that I'm doing it for a really fucking good reason that I don't yet have the skill or ability to write my way out of. Because though our stories may be fiction, the people who read them are not.

So now you may ask, What if it eviscerates my story if I take it out, the way you killed yours back at your writing workshop?

How we respond when someone tells us a trope or a story is problematic, or that we must take responsibility for it, is vitally important. It doesn't always mean "Burn it all down." It means this piece is broken and needs to be addressed. And if you're will-ing to live with that broken piece, it means owning up to it, saying yes, I know it's damaging to people, and I own that. Are you willing to do that? There have been subsequent instances where I was willing to put things in my novels—the abuse of a young man, a violent cutter—that I knew would turn off a lot of people to my work and could contribute to a larger problem of representation. But I felt they were vital to the story; eliminating them would have turned the story into a shiny, faceless marble.

Writers cry "Censorship!" when readers and reviewers point out issues like these, but the reality is that writers can write whatever they like. They simply need to take responsibility for it. They need to be able to sleep at night with a full understanding of what their choices have contributed to, and the world they are helping to build.

So, what world are you willing to build? How will you sleep at night? These are questions you should be asking with every keystroke.

Unpacking the "Real Writers Have Talent" Myth

I TAUGHT A COPYWRITING CLASS A FEW YEARS AGO, WHICH isn't something you'd generally ever see me doing. Classrooms aren't for me. Public appearances are exhausting, and teaching a class is one long song-and-dance routine. Afterward, you're so beat you need to recoup for a week and then do it all over again.

But what I loved about this opportunity was that I could impart some wisdom to folks about how to actually *make money writing*. One of the things that astonished me, once I got into marketing and advertising, is that nobody had ever thought to tell me I could write copy for a living and . . . actually . . . live on that money. It was always, "Hey, you can teach English or wait tables or do admin work while you write your books on the side and just be poor."

It turns out selling stuff with words is actually a skill our nutty consumerist culture really, really values.

Very few people can communicate well, and fewer still can do that in writing. I'd gotten a head start in my teens with pounding out sentences so, by the time I reached my midtwenties, I had some raw skills that I could hone on the job.

When I first started throwing together copy, I wasn't really sure what I was doing. I hadn't been trained. I was just blindly groping along, often referring to great ad campaigns I liked (Chipotle!) and studying their techniques. Every time I was given something to write I'd never written before (radio ads! TV ads! executive bios!) I hit up Google and read example after example after example, the same way I'd read books to get an idea of how to write a book.

It fact, it wasn't until the last few years, when I signed on to be an in-house writer with a global company, that I felt like I really started to figure out what the hell I was doing. This had to do with a couple things: the sheer volume of work, and the fact that we tracked the effectiveness of every campaign.

Writing so many pieces—and being able to adjust subsequent pieces to the same audience if the numbers that come back are bad—had a profound effect on how I viewed myself as a writer. Before that, I was writing things and throwing them out there and hoping that something stuck. And lots of folks just went, "Okay, looks good," because most folks don't know how to write either.

One of the most valuable things for my career, though, was teaching that copywriting class. I'm a big believer in the idea that writing can be taught, because at its heart, basic writing-to-be-understood is just a formula, and you can teach formulas. It's just harder for some people to pick up than others. And the people who have a rough time have to work a lot harder.

To do this I had to figure out my actual process and then communicate it to other people. It forced me to turn a critical eye on some of my favorite ads, and figure out why some worked and why some didn't. I also increased my reading of other successful copywriters. Reading them gave me ways to talk about things I already did but didn't have a name for.

Ads are actually really simple formulas: Promise (You will be happy if you buy Coke!), Proof (All of these people are happy and they drink Coke!), Price ($4.99 for a twelve-pack! Here's a coupon for $1 off!). Or, Problem (Got acne?), Solution (We can cure your acne!), Call to Action (Call 1-800-ACNE today!). I'd go so far as so say every successful ad adheres to this sort of formula—with some variations for length, like the addition of further proof points—but it wasn't something I was explicitly taught, it was something I absorbed with constant practice. I remember what a revelation it was to realize there were names for these things. Maybe I should have spent actual time studying how to be a copywriter before I wrote copy, but looking back over my school career, I couldn't recall even one class that taught copywriting. It was just something you were expected to pick up or not. Which is like asking somebody to just "pick up" algebra.

Studying copywriters and teaching these things to others helped me codify my own process, so that when I started to get overwhelmed by a project, or flailed, I could just go back to basics. I had this feeling the other morning, when I sat down to write yet another email for the same product, to the same audience. The emails have been doing all right, but just sending these folks the same thing they've been getting isn't going to connect with the people who didn't connect with the last message. I realized I needed to go back to the beginning of the process again—research into the product and the target audience—to see if I could glean any new approaches to the same material. You have to look for pain points (the problem) and product benefits (the solution) and think of new and interesting ways to communicate those in a way that's compelling.

It's a challenge, and I like challenges.

The experience of teaching myself to write marketing copy is one reason why I always rankle when people tell me that writing can't be taught—that you just have it ("it" being talent or something) or you don't.

Which is pretty much bullshit.

I was reading an "aspiring" writer's blog the other day where they went on and on about how writing is really pointless because there are so many other people in the world more talented than them, and they'll have to work so hard to be even half as good, and I was like, "Yeah, so? So you have to work hard. Suck it up and do the work."

Because when I hear people talk about "talent," what I interpret them saying is that writing just comes more easily to some people than other people and that means only people who find it "easy" should even try. Most often, though, "talent" exists because 1) that person enjoys writing, and because they enjoy writing, they've been doing it years and years longer than other people. Only very occasionally does it mean 2) figuring out how to write a book required very little actual effort because they easily grokked the form after a few passes.

We've all met those folks who just breezed through math class or sat at a piano and figured it out easily and could play in a few weeks what took somebody else a few years. But looking at the careers of my peers and colleagues, what I see is a lot of hard work. Millions upon millions of words of hard work and discipline. Is it easier for some writers to write amazing stuff or complete a book than it is for me? *Absolutely*. But you know what that means? It means I just have to work harder to be as good, or as fast, or put together a better sentence. And instead of seeing that as a roadblock or some discouraging shit, I see it as a huge challenge.

And I like challenges.

I remember living in Chicago and getting a rejection slip from Ellen Datlow, the then–senior editor of *Sci Fiction* magazine and one of the foremost editors in the field. It was the end of a really long day and I slid to the floor in the kitchen and sobbed my eyes out. I was so tired. So, so tired of writing story after story. The problem with my short story writing, I would later learn, was that I didn't actually like short stories, and didn't read many of them. Which made writing them a bit difficult, and I wasn't "naturally talented" enough to pick it up after reading just a few. But after many, many years, I sold some more stories. And then some books. Because I didn't take every rejection slip as a blow to my inherent "talent." I took it as a sign that I had to work harder.

A lot fucking harder.

I can punch out a pretty decent marketing email these days, but I had to write nearly a thousand of them to get that good. And novels? *God's War* was the third novel I tried to sell and the ninth I'd ever written, and it was rejected and cancelled many times. When I talk to other writers and find out they sold the first book they ever wrote—or, my favorite author story, "I totally came up with this idea for a novel when I was getting high with my friends, wrote it in a year or so, and a publisher paid me five figures for it! It was pretty cool!"—I want to bang my head on my desk.

But the truth is, writing a book that *I* thought was good and a publisher/the marketplace thought was good took me a *fucking long time*. And a lot of failure. Continual failure. And every time I failed I'd rage at the world and then suck it up and *try harder*.

Because you only really fail when you give up.

So to read people ranting on about talent and how some writers "have it" and some writers don't just makes me roll my eyes, because it sounds like something you say to discourage people; worse, it sounds like some kind of ancient "blood will tell" bullshit, like writing success is wholly based on genetics.

Double bullshit.

If I'd given up writing marketing copy after my first email, or just said to my boss, "Sorry, I don't know how to write radio ads. You'll need to get someone else," I wouldn't be where I am in my day job.

If you suck at writing, suck it up.

The world is full of people who write poorly but passionately, and others who can put a sentence together but have no feeling behind it. All they have in common is that they don't give up when people say they're talentless hacks. And both of those types of writers have audiences.

I'm a believer that writing can be taught—hence the reason I taught that copywriting class—but you also have to *want* to be good at it. If you say to me, "Well, I'd like to be a lawyer, but I don't have the talent for it," then I'm most likely to tell you that you just don't want to be a lawyer all that badly. (If you say you don't have the money, that's a whole other issue entirely.)

You either want it, or you don't. You either put the time in, or you don't.

So don't tell me you're "not as good" as Margaret Atwood or Elizabeth Bear or Mary Renault.

You're goddamn right you're probably not "as good" as somebody who's been writing a decade, two decades, six decades longer than you, every day, often to the point of injury.

Don't tell me you don't have talent, or somebody else has more. That's just an excuse. If you want it, suck it up and *work harder*. Because that's all this business is.

GEEK

Some Men Are More Monstrous Than Others: On *True Detective*'s Men and Monsters

WHEN I WAS SIXTEEN, I DATED A GUY WITH A MADONNA/ whore complex. I had no idea what that was, at the time, being a young woman from a rural town where belittling women as sluts and whores was pretty typical. You were either "the type of woman men married" or you were . . . well, probably a slut. All I knew was that when he talked about me, he said I was some transformative goddess, superior to all other women—smarter, and sexier—and all other women he spoke about were bitches or whores. He disrespected his mother and grandmother—got into screaming fights with them and belittled them. He had no female friends. I took him for a poor abused and misdirected kid too smart for his own good.

Boys who backlashed were to be pitied and sympathized with. They'd just had rough lives. You needed to sympathize with them—and I could, I really could, because the world was filled with stories of men who'd had hard times, and who lashed out at others because of it. I had a fistful of excuses, as did he. We had a narrative on TV, in the movies. Men ran after you and screamed and got upset because they loved you. Men were abusive, maybe, even . . . because they loved you.

We know this story.

What first really bothered me, though, was when he made fun of a former friend of mine because she was fat. That might seem weird, after all this other behavior. But the reason it bugged me is because as he sneered over her being another man's "fat girlfriend" I couldn't help noting that she was, in fact, thinner than me.

His extreme complimentariness toward me had nothing to do with me—setting me up as a singular goddess was his way of justifying his relationship with me. Because if all women were bitches and whores, the fact that he was in a relationship with a woman must mean I was something different. Something else. So he made me into something I wasn't: a perfect picture of womanhood. A crowned goddess.

But woe to the goddess who falls.

Needless to say, a perfect picture of womanhood I was not, and have never been. Things began to fall apart in the typical way they do when these sorts of guys finally wheedle you away from family and friends. When we moved in together, a five-hour drive away from our hometown, things got pretty bad. Not that they were candy before—I tried to break up with him three times during the two years of our courtship prior to us moving in together, once because he cheated on me, and twice more for outbursts of screaming temper. But then came the weeping, the apologizing, about how he was imperfect and I was a goddess, and could I please just give him another chance. . . .

Once we moved in together the swing between these behaviors became more extreme. There would be screaming fights. He'd throw things. I put on a bunch of weight and started wearing frumpy clothes, secretly hoping this would finally be the thing that got him to break up with me. When that didn't work, I actually hit him on the shoulder once, during a fight, hoping he'd hit me back and I could justify leaving him. I contemplated suicide—anything to get out.

In the end, he joined the military to spite his grandmother, who'd cut off his money for college, and the break gave me the chance to call up my parents and move back home. When he returned from boot camp, we went round again for a few weeks, trying to "be friends." When that didn't work, the threats started.

So I understand the problems inherent in being someone's crowned goddess. In part, it's this empathy that made the first season of *True Detective* so riveting for me. *True Detective*'s first season takes us on a journey across the poor, rural South of the '90s—when I was a teen—following an odd-couple cop duo as they track an occult serial killer targeting women and children. The first body they turn up is a woman given a tangled crown of deer antlers by her killer. I could see where this was going to go.

I'm pretty burned out on murder shows featuring slog after slog of dead women, but the weirdness of the opening murder, paired with the bromancing odd couple played by Woody Harrelson and Matthew McConaughey, intrigued me.

There are a number of things to praise in this show, from a storytelling perspective. The narrative jumps between events occurring in 1995, 2002, and 2012 in a way that's skillfully done. The writing is superb. Even television shows that I'd say were "excellent" aren't this narratively ambitious. Unlike traditional network TV and even some of its fellow HBO programming, *True Detective* trusts viewers to connect the dots; it invites us to take a leap of faith.

I was amused to see a little of my own grim humor in the character of the introverted and this-world-is-fucked-up Rust, played by Matthew McConaughey, but the character that made me laugh out loud was Marty, played by Woody Harrelson.

Why Marty? Because, as I said to my spouse during episode two or three, "Holy crap! I *dated* that guy!"

My spouse looked appropriately horrified, because though it's one thing to hear about a thing, it's another thing to see it. Watching Marty neatly box up different aspects of his life, telling lies about how he lives and his morals and believing them while cavorting with young women and putting his wife on a pedestal, was oddly cathartic, for me, because it was a validation that these types of people exist, and they are, indeed, their own brand of monstrous.

True Detective is a bromance at its core—if you think this is not a romance story, I challenge you to watch that scene in the monster's lair at the end, when Marty is reaching out to Rust and then cradles him in his lap, and you tell me that's not some Greek hero romance shit. It's a story of men incapable of living in the very society they purport to protect.

But unlike Marty, Rust understands his own monstrousness. He understands he's had to become evil to fight evil.

Marty continues to think his behavior is normal, and he is rewarded for it, even partially pardoned by his family with a lukewarm reunion there at the end in his hospital room.

True Detective's failure is the same failure of its heroes—a failure of empathy for and acknowledgment of the humanity and autonomy of the very women and children these men insist they are here to protect from men far more monstrous than themselves.

Marty's inability to draw this line—if it was not made clear before—was made crystalline at the very end of the series, when he does finally end up fucking the former sixteen-year-old prostitute he handed a few hundred dollars to seven years before to help her get out of that life. Rust snarkily said at the time, "That a down payment?" and, of course, it turns out that it is.

Where the show pulls its punches with Marty, here, is by making the girl the instigator of this relationship, later on in the show. It doesn't have the balls to make Marty the one pursuing her, though it would have been a much more narratively accurate choice. It wouldn't surprise me if it were Harrelson himself who rewrote this bit to make Marty more likable—by painting the woman as the primary problem. By perpetuating this narrative of the sexy lady instigator, Marty is painted as an irresponsible child who can't resist the flirtatious temptations of a twenty-three-year-old former prostitute. What man can control his dick, amirite? (Counterpoint: *Twin Peaks'* Agent Cooper.[1]) But however much they try to wiggle out of this one, the text is still there. The women in Marty's life are virgins and whores—his wife and everyone else.

When he loses his shit at his mistress for telling his wife of their affair, his true nature becomes apparent. Even more than trying to control who his mistress dates and bursting into her home unannounced to beat up the guy she brought home, it was the screaming phone conversation where he says, "I'm going to skullfuck you!" that really peeled back the layers of affable family man to reveal the raging, poisonous monster beneath.

Rust, by contrast, understands his own darker impulses. His backstory is not a frigid wife, interestingly enough, but a frigid daughter; I expected laziness here where his whole family would have gone out in a flaming wreck, but it was more telling that he lost a child through accident, but a wife through an inability to cope. When he goes off the rails and becomes a horror, he recognizes that he's not fit to associate with the very women and children he's chasing after serial killers to protect.

He has no illusions of what he is.

Pulling his punches does not make him any less of a monster. This is brilliantly illustrated again and again, but in particular in his fight with Marty, when he lets Marty beat the shit out of him, right up until the very end. Years before, he once grabbed hold of Marty's hands and told him how he would break them, and now he grabs hold of his wrists, expression set, and you know he is going to carry through on this threat now. You know he's going to break Marty's wrists. You see the death grip. You see the monster in his eyes. You see Marty is about to never be able to hold a gun again. And then a group of other men pulls Rust away, and Marty keeps his hands.

Monsters wrangling monsters.

We are also not fooled after watching the crazy shoot-out in the projects when Rust teams up with a biker gang to assault the house of a drug dealer in a predominantly black neighborhood. What starts out as a robbery quickly turns into the terrorization of an entire community as the firefight rages across the neighborhood and the police move in. Though he is given his "save the cat" moment by sparing a young boy in the house they're robbing by telling him to hide in the bathtub instead of shooting him, and though he tries to incapacitate instead of brutally murder the neighborhood folks as they try to defend themselves, it's clear he knows exactly what he is, and exactly what he's capable of.

I have always had an obsession with the monsters who walk among us—the ones our society excuses and supports, especially. I'm interested in the narrative that to fight monsters, you must, necessarily, become one.

Rust and Marty spend their lives limping along, trying to find ways to live in civilized society as casual monsters, but in the end—as shown in the brief and sadly funny roundup of how they're living their lives in the present right before their final fight—they have failed at it.

Marty sits at home alone eating TV dinners in front of the

tube, divorced and estranged from his daughters. Rust spent seven years working at a bar four days a week, and drinking himself senseless the other three. All they know how to do is fight monsters, because they know monsters. They understand them. They are uniquely equipped to fight them.

Because they are monstrous.

I've said often that there's a difference between a show that portrays misogyny and a show that is misogynist. *Mad Men* portrays misogyny. *True Detective*, sadly, is misogynist. It paints the world in the viewpoint of its monstrous heroes, so I suppose it shouldn't be any wonder that it comes out that way. But here's what makes the difference, for me:

Marty's wife, Maggie, tries to leave him, again and again. She asks Rust if Marty is having an affair—Rust knows he is, but protects Marty (remember, this is a bromance). Eventually the mistress confronts her, and she packs up her shit and leaves Marty for a few months.

But I know Marty. I dated Marty. I know this dance. And they have kids. Kids make it harder.

He woos her back. He gets down on his knees. He sweet-talks and apologizes. He makes small concessions. They go to therapy. He quits drinking. But as his daughters grow up, we see his controlling nature rear its head again; he beats up the men having sex with his daughter. He calls her a slut. He pokes at her choice of clothing in a particularly amusing scene in which she tells him with the haughty voice of a disgruntled teen, "You can't control what women wear, Dad."

And, years later, he has another affair. This time, Maggie knows. This time, she calls Rust again for confirmation. Rust again pretends ignorance.

Maggie knows she needs to leave Marty. She knows she needs something besides "you're having an affair," because she knows how things will go. He'll get on his knees. He'll apologize. He'll make excuses.

But there's one thing he won't stand for: another man touching what he considers his. She has spent her life wrangling this monster. She knows him intimately. She understands what she must do to beat him. So she endeavors to have an affair. She tries to pick up a man at a bar, but that's too impersonal. She knows her husband well, knows how he thinks, and knows exactly what will hurt him most and end their relationship with no blubbering apologies and promises to do better. Instead she gets drunk and hunts down Rust and convinces him to have sex with her.

I knew exactly why she'd chosen to do as she did, and I understood it. I knew she was right. I'd been there; boxed into a corner, unable to figure out how to get away. In the end, I hadn't had kids. I'd been able to pack up my shit and move to Alaska.

Maggie didn't have that luxury.

So Maggie has a quick coupling with Rust.

Afterwards, when she sits at the kitchen table with her glass of wine, waiting for Marty at home in the dark, she is finally supremely confident. Because she knows this will wreck him. She knows, after all this time, she finally got him. Because she understands exactly what she is to him—a possession—and that the only way to bust herself down from that pedestal he put her on is to paint herself as a whore.

I hated Maggie for this as much as anyone, which was shocking. I *knew* Maggie. But the narrative! Oh, we know the narrative of the woman who ruins everything. Marty and Rust battle it out, naturally, after this incident, and are no longer friends. It feels like grim trickery for her to do it, and it is. But I completely understood her, and I sympathized with her. I knew she'd made the choice she felt was the only choice to free her from her situation; she'd done something awful, to escape something worse.

But I wondered, the way this whole mess was painted—how many others saw what she did as I had? How many others really sympathized with her situation? How many actually considered her a scheming whore, just the way Marty did?

Because when she shows up at the end of the show to see Rust, even knowing what I did, sympathizing as I did, I hated her. I hated that she'd hurt his feelings. I had to remind myself that she had, in part, also lashed out to hurt Rust because he'd known from the start that Marty was having affairs, and he'd lied to her about it. He'd protected Marty, and this was the most powerful way this fucked-up, misogynist world had given Maggie to say "fuck you."

It occurred to me that in a world ruled by misogynist monsters, they end up pushing people into becoming the very stereotypes they've created in their own minds. I flashed back to the gun fight in the projects—the four white men with guns terrorizing the neighborhood, getting them to fight back, and the cops and helicopters that swoop in. I imagined the scene in the minds of the cops who descended on the scene: "Those violent black people," they'd say, when it was white thugs who'd instigated the violence in the first place.

Through force, abuse of physical and social power, and neglect, these men perpetuate the very narratives they've created in their heads. They've made the world they imagined, and it's a very terrible place.

Much of the initial furor over the first season of *True Detective* centered around the inclusion of occult aspects of the show. Just how much was it going to incorporate the hinted-at Cthulhu mythos, including referencing *The King in Yellow*, the weird fiction classic? In the end, it didn't deliver on this for a lot of folks, and I think that's because they missed what it is really about. This is a story about human monsters. It's a show set in a fantasy world, but not the one people expected. It's a fantasy world as painted by two broken men who strive to extinguish a greater darkness than themselves in order to atone for and justify the darkness they themselves have delivered into the world.

If there was ever a show that so accurately represented that old cliché "women take up with men to protect them from other men," this is it. What *True Detective* makes clear is that that saying could just as easily be "women must take up with monsters to protect them from other monsters."

It is for this reason that the show's final lines, delivered by Marty, hold a different meaning than the obvious one.

Rust says that when you look up in the sky, all is darkness, and the darkness is winning. Marty disagrees because, of course, in the beginning there was only darkness, and now the sun comes up again. So to his mind, light is making a fair bit of progress.

For me, this was not so much a glorious mythic hand wave to the great literal battle between light and darkness, but the figurative one: the battle between darkness and light that goes on inside everyone, especially men, given the power these two wield—the gun and the badge, the sword and the scales.

Power is a funny thing, because if you asked these two men if they had it, they would say no. They would say they were underdogs fighting a corrupt system.

But when you pull back—when you see Marty abuse prisoners and call his teen daughter a slut, and Rust cover up the shooting of a handcuffed man and sneer at Maggie—you recognize that their whole lives have been about fighting darkness to cover up their own, and raging at powerful men because those men treat them the same way they treat their wives and daughters. You understand that they cannot stand for enduring that type of abuse from powerful men. They cannot be made women in their own world.

The body they saw posed in the cane fields that day did not evoke their sympathy because it was the death of a human being, a woman. No, it bothered them because in it they saw the work of a man who believed himself to be more powerful than they, playing out a battle of wits on women's bodies, as so many wars between monsters have been waged.

On reflection, looking at shows like this and considering my own experiences, what fascinated me was that we have so many stories like this that help us empathize with monstrous men. "Yes, these men are flawed, but they are not as evil as *this* man." Even more chilling, they tend to be stories that paint women as roadblocks, aggressors, antagonists, complications—but only in the context of them being a bitch, a whore, a Madonna. The women are never *people*.

Stories about monstrous men are not meant to teach us how to empathize with the women and children murdered, but with the men fighting over their bodies.

As a woman menaced by monsters, I find this particularly interesting, this erasure of me from a narrative meant to, if not justify, then explain the brokenness of men. There are shows much better at this, of course, which don't paint women out of the story—*Mad Men* is the first to come to mind, and *Game of Thrones*—but *True Detective* doubled down.

The women terrorized by monsters in real life are active agents. They are monster-slayers, monster-pacifiers, monster-nurturers, monster-wranglers—and some of them are monsters, too. In truth, if we are telling a tale of those who fight monsters, it fascinates me that we are not telling more women's stories, as we've spun so many narratives like *True Detective* that so blatantly illustrate the sexist masculinity trap that turns so many human men into the very things they despise.

Where are the women who fight them? Who partner with

them? Who overcome them? Who battle their own monsters to fight greater ones?

Because I have and continue to be one of those women, navigating a horror show world of monsters and madmen. We are women who write books and win awards and fight battles and carve out extraordinary lives from ruin and ash. We are not background scenery, our voices silenced, our motives and methods constrained to sex.

I cannot fault the show's men for forgetting that; they've created the world as they see it. But I can prod the show's exceptional writers, because in erasing the narrative of those whose very existence is constantly threatened by these monsters, including trusted monsters whose natures vacillate wildly, they sided with the monsters.

I'm not a bit player in a monster's story. But with narratives like this perpetuated across our media, it wouldn't surprise me if that's how my obituary read: a catalogue of the men who sired me, and fucked me, and courted me.

Stories that are not my own.

Funny, isn't it? The power of story.

It's why I picked up a pen.

I slay monsters, too.

Die Hard, Hetaerae,
and Problematic Pin-Ups:
A Rant

THE UBIQUITOUS PIN-UP CALENDAR HAS SERVED AS A fundraiser for several charities run by science fiction and fantasy writers—including the Clarion Writers' Workshop. These projects left me with a deep feeling of unease, but it wasn't until I started putting the pieces together about why I thought they were problematic that I understood why the pin-up calendar as professional fundraising project really bothered me.

I watch *Die Hard* at least a couple of times a year; it's one of the best-written films out there. But there were always two moments in the film that confounded me from the very start, even when I watched it as a kid. There's a moment when John Mc-Clane is upstairs in the floors under construction, and he's trying to figure out how to get the attention of the police even though the phone lines are cut. During this high-tension scene, the camera's attention swoops with John's to the building across the way, where a naked woman is talking on the phone, and the camera holds there for a few seconds while he watches her, openmouthed. Right after this moment, he hits the fire alarm to call the authorities, so I figured that somehow this scene was meant to show us his thought processes—Hey, other people in the buildings next door have phones. What other way do we have to communicate?—in addition to being a general male-gazey moment for the audience.

But on actually reading the script recently, I found that this scene was in fact meant to be nothing more than what it is— John checking out a naked lady on the phone in the next building. It wasn't supposed to lead to some other revelation. It wasn't the bridge scene between "What do I do?" and "Pull the fire alarm."

It was just a dude watching a naked woman.

There's another interesting moment that happens as McClane is running around the rooftop of the building. At one point he cuts through a locker room, and there's a *Playboy* pin-up on the wall. He is literally being chased by people with guns, and he slows down and takes a moment to appreciate the pin-up. Later, he goes so far as to pat the pin-up again—for luck, presumably?—as his situation continues to deteriorate.

Die Hard is an '80s movie, one with a core emotional conflict that centered on real social change happening at the time— women moving into executive positions and beginning to out-earn their husbands. Where was the place for men, in a world like that? How did you define being a man, when it wasn't through being a breadwinner? What did it mean to be a dude when there were no more monsters to fight and your wife was a CEO?

This is where the film doubles down on John McClane's masculinity. Not only is he a tough cop with the skills to protect his wife from "real" danger (as opposed to corporate mergers), but he's a red-blooded type of man with a healthy, lusty drive for women. He is not, the film insists, henpecked or submissive or cuckolded or unmanned in any way by his financially more powerful wife. These little nods—however odd, within the context of the actual narrative, which is a dude being chased through a tower by terrorists—that show him participating in the "normal" objectification of women are meant, I think, to be reassuring.

Weirdly.

Just as a soldier in WWII would paint a lusty pin-up on his plane, or have it folded up in his jacket, McClane both acknowledges and pats his own, for luck. She is not meant to be a real person, of course. The real person—the problematic, complicated person—is his wife. The pin-up is the easy stand-in: something easily controlled, always there, reassuring. Pin-ups are objectifications of people—people who can be owned and called upon whenever the viewer needs them. They exist as things, and they exist primarily for one purpose.

Context is important when we choose to make a piece of art. Knowing and understanding how our piece of art will be read or viewed within the historical context of other pieces of art is vital both to understanding how others will read it and to formulating the defense of our choice despite that context. As someone who wrote a very violent series of novels featuring a cast of characters who use Arabic words on occasion, I'm pretty familiar with the importance of this process.

Context, or lack thereof, was one of the reasons I found the notion of the pin-up calendar as fundraising initiative[1] really noxious and depressing. Because despite the many posts I would see from folks defending it (folks hopping in and feeling there was a need to defend it before it had even been made spoke volumes right off the bat) and the fact that the latest one was, in fact, in support of the Clarion Writers' Workshop, the project wasn't going to escape being seen within the history of the pin-up. No matter how much everyone wished it.

And that's what I saw. How those images have been used, by whom, and for what purpose.

But I avoided the discussion around it at the time, because wasn't it obvious? Was it really worth my spoons?

The "pin-up" dates back to the late 1800s, and was a form of marketing used for dancers and actresses. It's interpreted by some as a rather rebellious act, flying in the face of Victorian sensibilities related to women's place in the home, as opposed to in the public sphere. But it was not always the actress or dancer herself who created the pin-up, and as much as folks want to hang a hat on it being somehow "empowering," I'll note that it was, in fact, just a form of marketing. It was actresses and dancers all dolled up, looking their best, selling their performances based on their charming good looks; much of it just as stuffed, primped, and polished up as the worst Photoshop of our day. The pin-up was problematic already upon its inception, as they certainly would have been reminiscent of pornography.

Faking bodily perfection to get along in a world in which women in particular were seen as consumer goods has a long and sordid history, too. Did you know women in ancient Athens of the hetaera class—who acted as companions and courtesans—actually stuffed their clothes so they looked like they had bigger breasts and butts? They bound and smoothed flabby bodies. They wore wigs when necessary. They faked it.

But why? Why all the faking? Why did women have to look perfect in person, or at least perfect in the marketed pin-up?

Because women, in many cultures—and in the history of many cultures—are seen as commodities. As objects. Their worth is measured in beauty. Whether you're selling me your idealized form of yourself or someone else is doing it, the sad fact is that pushing this type of fake bullshit on us is part of a larger history of commoditizing people—whether we are selling ourselves or being sold by others. And yes, people can be sexy in many different ways! That's true. People are sexy. But this type of representation of "sexy" doesn't look like actual bedtime sexiness any more than your typical porn movie actually looks like you and your partner(s) getting it on. It's a trick. It's marketing. It's meant to create a desire—for you to want, or to want to aspire to—that only the object can fulfill.

Of course, people have fucked and procreated quite happily, full of imperfections, for hundreds of thousands of years. But we are less good at celebrating that, or simply accepting it, than we are at rubbing away people's flaws and turning them into rock-god heroes we can all pretend we own, or pretend can be bought. Because there's not a lot of money in telling everyone they're attractive just as they are, or that a woman is not a thing one can own to soothe one's problems. People still want to believe there are women, in particular, who will serve all their wants and needs and give up being a complicated company CEO in order to do it.

This is really what the pin-up is about. It's about ownership. Inciting desire. Making people think they can own a thing by going out and seeing the actress at work, or hiring her for a show. It's selling the desire for ownership.

After coming off a long period researching slavery in antiquity for my new series, it's very difficult for me to go all rah-rah empowerment when I see folks trying to make perfection and/or forced subservience sexy. There's too much horrifying history behind that.

Rah-rah empowerment of this sort reminds me of the story of a "freed" woman named Neaera in Athens, a former prostitute whose "freedom" was actually bought by two of her most ardent suitors, whom she was required by law to split her time between, even though she was legally considered "free."[2] As lovely as it would be to think these folks had some kind of happy polyamorous union, or that they did this out of True Love, on reading the accounts of this particular transaction, she continued sleeping with them both from time to time (not living with them, but occasionally visiting them to have sex) because they effectively owned her; she was in debt to them. So she was "free," sure, but only free from being forced to have sex with a lot of people instead of just these two people. And oh, sure, it could indeed be more complicated than that. Stockholm syndrome, and all that. We often find ourselves in love with our oppressors, because otherwise we'd go mad. Maybe she even genuinely liked them. Maybe they liked her too, though I suspect that if that was the case, one of them would have married her, or helped her make a good living outside of fucking them.

This actually happened a lot in antiquity—men buying the "freedom" of a woman (and other men) and then continuing to have sex with them, only for "free." It creeped the ever-loving fuck out of me, as much of my research about Athens did, because as much as the U.S. school system holds up Athens as some kind of modern utopia, the truth is the top 1 percent of people were ruling over a vast, stratified society of people in various states of enslavement.

It's creepy as all get-out, these varying levels of body-ownership.

And in this society of enslavement and subservience, in a culture of people as things, slaves and hetaerae and the like also understood the importance of marketing. It's why they faked their looks with cosmetics and sewn-up hair and plush butts. Because they or their owners knew they were only as valuable as their perceived worth as sexual objects or, at least, desirable objects that the 1 percent could fight over.

I hadn't much thought about the annoying literary pin-up calendars in a while—not since Justin Landon at the book review blog *Staffer's Musings* brought it up again as being intensely problematic as a fundraising effort.[3] Yet it was one of those low-level annoyances I've learned to live with over the years. Why speak up about it being a problematic way to raise money—this selling of fictional women's bodies—when there were so many other problems in the world?

But one morning I clicked on a link to photos of a woman who'd undergone surgeries for three types of cancers. With clothes on, from the neck up, you'd assume she had the form of some privileged person, and of course, with clothes on, and with her thin frame and symmetrical features, she does likely enjoy a lot of privilege out in the big bad world.

But what she'd actually done was take her clothes off, not to be pin-up sexy, but to be real about what bodies that have survived three types of cancer actually look like. She'd had reconstructive surgery on her breasts, which were missing nipples. There was a broad scar across her belly. More scars on her legs, her arms; there was loose, stretched skin from rapid weight loss related to her illness. And though her face was as carefully made up as any pin-up's would be, her body showed us a much realer picture; her body carried the record of what she'd been through. Hers was the body of a person who'd been through the shit and survived it, not a body we were invited to own.

It was in staring at that picture that I became angry again at the idea that pin-up calendars were being used to support literary foundations. Because it was in that moment that the whole complicated hand-wringing I'd seen so many do in support of the calendar just fell apart for me.

We are selling fantasies.

As fantasists, as fiction writers, we sell fantasy. I get that. But fantasy is not bodies. It's stories. What we sell does not have to be in service to a narrative of objectification.

I don't sell stories about perfect people you can stack neatly on a shelf, anyway. I'd argue few writers actually do. I present flawed, angry, battered, busted, messed-up people who aren't here to be your fucking friends. They're not here to fulfill your desires. They are not here to be looked at, or owned. In truth, when I write "the end," I strive to ensure that all of my characters have a life that's going on beyond that last page, a life you might think about sometimes; you might wonder what they're up to. But it's not a life you own, any more than you own mine. It's a life you get to participate in for a while, maybe. But then they go home, and you go home.

When I started to try to figure out what a pin-up calendar of characters from my books would look like, I came up blank, because my characters aren't selling their bodies. They aren't meant to be singular sexual objects, or actresses (or actors). They're meant to be people. People who aren't owned.

What you'd end up with is something like Nyx—the foul-talking, head-chopping mercenary from my God's War series—sitting on the toilet, belly fat spilling out, ragged scars up her thighs, hairy legs splayed, spitting sen on the floor from a bruised mouth. She'd be sitting there with mismatched skin lined in scars and stretch marks and maybe paging through some boxing magazine, fuck-it-all, not interested in you, flabby breasts unbound and spilling onto her stomach. And she couldn't give a fuck about you. She's not interested in your problems, or patting you on the head, or giving you some bit of happy luck when you throw yourself from a rooftop crawling with German terrorists.

And that's just the one who doesn't give a toss for being naked. There are a million other characters who would spit in your face before posing as objects, to be drawn out and commoditized; it would mean rejecting everything they were, everything they believed in, to pose as some perfect, pawed-over item in a stranger's inventory. I tried to imagine Lilia, the primary protagonist in my new series, with her scarred face and clawed hand and bum leg, whose entire existence has been within a consent culture where people retain absolute autonomy over themselves and their bodies and their desires, getting pitched this idea, and I could just imagine her screwing up her face like, "You want what?"

Because make no mistake—pin-ups are created to cash in on the desires of others, from the very start. They are a marketing medium. They are meant to sell us idealized fantasy, perfect objects, things, and they do this by presenting people the same way we would a sexy new dishwasher or a succulent browned duck ready for the eating. "Here is something you can own," we say. "Something just for you."

And the bodies we present to them are flawless objects, beautifully rendered.

Own this. Be this. Do this.

But I'm not selling bodies. I'm selling stories.

Stories.

And just like that, after looking at that image that morning, I saw all the calendars we prop up, the calendars we go through such squirrelly mind-fucking doublethink to make "okay" and empowering. And I thought about how that let's-be-sexy-and-take-control-of-the-narrative talk was actually just another part of a fucked narrative. Just another example of presenting flawless bodies for easy consumption—instead of stories.

For all the back-bending work we do to defend our problematic choices, sometimes we're not actually working out how to save the world, or stop sexism, or empower women with pole dancing. And sometimes all we're really doing is being a dude watching a naked woman in the next building, biding our time until the next plot token arrives.

Wives, Warlords, and Refugees:
The People Economy of Mad Max

I WASN'T GOING TO GO AND SEE THE LATEST ITERATION of Mad Max, titled *Mad Max: Fury Road*.

Don't get me wrong: I'm a passionate fan of '80s apocalypse movies (I wrote a whole series in homage to them!). I love the aesthetics, the desperation, the tough characters, the monstrous masculinity that both men and women must take up in order to survive. But I've watched as the heroines of those gritty '80s epics I loved have been continually debased, ground out, and erased here in the last twenty years. When you're watching a film from 1979 that has tougher, more complex female characters than a film shot in 2012, something is rotten. (I'm looking at you, *Riddick*, with the director who argued that constant rape attempts, threats, and two-second "side boob with nipple" shots were actually a vitally important part of his artistic vision instead of just lazy storytelling.) I've seen the politics inherent in these types of stories get pushed aside in favor of mindless, disjointed action sequences and shiny creatures with no bearing on the human plot. These films and their writers and directors have forgotten the truism of the postapocalyptic world: every resource is valuable. Every person—and hence, every scene—has to pull their weight. Only the toughest or most valued survive. And the stories that we remember, the stories that last, are about people struggling to survive in the midst of overwhelming odds presented both by the landscape and by their fellow travelers.

There's a lot of whining about "message fiction" these days, which is bizarre because every story is a "message" story or it wouldn't be a story. Asking for "stories without messages" makes me think this is code for a steady diet of inane reality TV shows. Reality TV does actually have a message, folks. That message is selling and reinforcing capitalism, ignorance, and the status quo. The reality is that every story is political, and the stories that stick with me best are incredibly and transparently so. There's a reason we remember *Animal Farm*, and *A Canticle for Leibowitz*, and *Nineteen Eighty-Four*. There's a reason I can't stop thinking about *Parable of the Sower*. Postapocalyptic stories have always had a lot to say about where we're headed if we don't right our wrongs. They warn us about our reliance on fossil fuels, our abuse of the environment, and where those will lead us. They tell us about the inevitable future we are building by relying on war, and what our continued reliance on slavery as an economic system means for our humanity. Postapocalypse stories simply do not exist without politics.

I knew *Mad Max: Fury Road* was headed in the right direction from the beginning, when Imperator Furiosa, the right hand of tyrant Immortan Joe, conspires to help his wives escape servitude. When Immortan Joe realizes Imperator Furiosa has gone rogue, he runs to open up a great vault door. I knew immediately what he hoped to find behind that vault door. He is going to check up on his most valuable possessions. His possessions are people with the ability to have babies. When you are living in a postapocalyptic world of poisoned fertility and scarce resources, controlling the people who can have babies is of the utmost importance.

Those who can bear them are the means of that production. Gain control over the means of production, and you can rule the world.

And this is where this film gets all the violence-against-women stuff right, because it boldly and frankly positions it for what it is, stripping it of the male gaze, of sexuality, of uncontrollable male urges. There are no on-screen rape threats, rape attempts, or rapes because they would detract from the entire point. You have to strip all that away to see it for what it is: Sexism is about power. Sexism is about controlling the means of production.

At its core, sexism has very little to do with the act of sex.

It's why we see a large room full of well-fed women hooked up to milking machines—yes, milking machines—because all anybody drinks in this world is water and milk, and all you ever see them eat is bugs and lizards. The animals are dead. That leaves us with those women. And these women are owned totally and completely by Immortan Joe, who controls all the means of production—he owns the water and the women.

And, once he owns those two things, he owns *everyone and everything*. He has consolidated absolute power by turning people into chattel.

In this world, those who can bear babies are chattel, used to breed more soldiers and provide life-sustaining milk to the elite. They are fodder used in production of more fodder.

Max (who really is actually crazy in this one—not angry, but crazy) himself is chattel—captured and kept alive as a "blood bag" to give a much-needed blood transfusion to soldiers who are diseased and dying. He is fodder to fuel the soldiers of the war.

Immortan Joe's war boys themselves are chattel, bred and raised in a religion that celebrates their sacrifice in battle. They are fodder for the war machine.

"We are just the same," says Splendid, one of Immortan Joe's escaped wives, to Nux, a rogue war boy. The people in power want them both to believe that they are things, owned and driven to just one purpose.

Women and soldiers are just the same, manipulated by the same terrible elite into sacrificing their bodies for some rich man's cause. "We are not things" the wives have written on the walls of the prison where they are kept.

We live in a world that has made people into things. In Max's world, there's just no finery on top of it. There's nothing to shield you from it. The only medium to convince those in this world otherwise is religion, and religion is used again and again within this world to illustrate how it can help manipulate and control while giving purpose and hope. For mangled, dying boys in the desert, the hope of Valhalla gives comfort.

And this brings us to Furiosa, our hero. For as most folks who have seen prior Mad Max movies know, Max just sort of wanders into these weird enclaves, fucks around, and then wanders out. He is the traveler, the witness to their stories. And in just that way, he stumbles into Furiosa's story, this huge complex thing that's clearly been planned out for a long time and is already set into furious motion.

Max is not the hero. He's the witness. Just like the war boys yelling at one another "Witness me!" he is the one who goes on, who drags on. He is that wandering '80s apocalypse male hero, tied to nothing and no one. He has to be, so he can wander off at the end—as he inevitably does here—and leave the real heroes to deal with the messy business of mopping up and governing a new world.

Casting Charlize Theron as Furiosa was an astonishing choice, and I honestly had no idea she was in this film until a few days before it came out. I remember Ridley Scott giving an interview once where he said he hired the very best actors he could find for *Alien* so that he could give his full attention to the creature part, because he knew the creature part was going to be the toughest. It felt like Miller did a similar thing here—with so many incredible action sequences to film, he needed great actors in place who could work with very little dialogue. And Theron does that here in such a powerful, heartbreaking way that I found myself in awe of how she was able to communicate so much in a glance. There's this moment when she reenters her war rig after Max drives it away from an attacking motorcycle gang, and she looks him up and down as he scoots over, and she has this tiny . . . not smile, but almost approving or knowing glance that lets us know that she knows she's won him over, and he'll be on their side now. There are tons of moments like this throughout, where all we get is Theron's eyes to tell us everything, and they do, and it's extraordinary.

There's another amazing thing that happens in this movie that few people have commented on, and that I want to point out, and that's the lack of the pervy camera. We know the pervy camera. It's the camera that zooms in on women's asses and legs and torsos and sexualizes their bodies, like the camera itself is licking them up for the male viewer. We see this in every movie from *Transformers* to *Sucker Punch* to *Bounty Killer* to *Grindhouse*. It's become so ubiquitous that I remember watching the end of *Gravity*, where the camera pans around behind Sandra Bullock's butt, and I was like, "Oh God, please no," and I was surprised, actually surprised, that the camera shot her the way it would in an actual serious film that was filming a male character instead of the way it would film a woman in a softcore porn movie. And George Miller—for all that he dresses the rebel wives in white muslin bikinis—does not shoot any softcore porn here. Max stumbles onto them while they're washing themselves off with a hose, and while it's a striking scene after all that sand and violence, it's not porny. These women are washing themselves like practical people, not male sex fantasies, and the camera captures them that way. Even when the film has the opportunity for a full-frontal female nude shot—with the motorcycle matriarchy member sitting up on the broken electric pole as bait—it demurs. This is a rated R movie, but nudity is not necessary to the story.

Hear that, HBO? There is no gratuitous nudity in this story. It doesn't need it. So it doesn't include it.

And I'm not even going to bother going into the motorcycle matriarchy, because what else needs to be said here? But my god, motorcycle matriarchy, where have you been all my life?

I do want to say a little something about the mass of refugees bowing and scraping in the dirt beneath the towers of Immortan Joe, begging for water. This may have been the oddest world-building break in the movie for me. (I can totally buy the metal war guitar guy, honestly.) Because here we have this mass of refugees, but they don't seem to be serving any real purpose. They are not working—are they meant to be doing mining of some kind? Or are they literally just the masses camped out hoping for scraps? How do they serve the war machine? Is there a Soylent Green solution here that we're missing? And, because their absence was really noticeable—where are all the black people in the future? If this is meant to be far-future Australia, where are all the Asian people, and the Aborigines? I could count the numbers of both among the secondary and even background characters on one hand, which was another weird world-building break.

Sigh.

It occurs to me I have not touched much on Furiosa here, but what is there to say? She's the hero of the show, the warrior queen, the one with the grit and fortitude to bust five women out of prison and go riding off into the desert in search of a hazy half memory of a place. She is the one who must ultimately make the decision whether to ride across the desert or to turn back and fight Immortan Joe. All Max can do is suggest it. The entire agency of this entire film rests entirely in her hands.

And it's that agency that really makes this such a fine film for me, and one I'd call feminist waaaaay before I'd call something like *Jupiter Ascending* feminist. Because the entire story isn't about things that *happen* to Furiosa. It's about what Furiosa does with what has happened to her. I have heard all sorts of ideas about Furiosa's backstory, but listen—Furiosa is in this because she, too, needs redemption. She has propped up this guy's patriarchy her whole life. She has been complicit in letting these other women act as breeders, a fate that for whatever reason she was able to avoid—whether because she could not get pregnant or because she was just too valuable as an imperator, or both. And in taking on the role she did, she was part of the problem. She upheld Immortan Joe's rule. It was time for her to earn her redemption. She drives this narrative hard and fast, and nothing happens without her having to make a decision about it. She's in charge of her own story.

Our rebel wives also get plenty to do in this film. Unlike so many heroines hanging off the side of a male character, it's clear in this world that not pulling your weight will get you dead very quickly, and these women fight in a way that is realistic to how they were raised. No, they aren't out doing kung fu, but they are hitting people with tools, using chains to haul Max off Furiosa, counting out bullets, scouting ahead, helping to get the truck unstuck, and all other manner of things that people do in a world where they're on the run and their very survival is at stake. No one survives and escapes sexual slavery and then gets upset at the idea of breaking a nail while hooking up a winch, for God's sake, though so many films would have you think otherwise. In truth, my only nitpick here is that they clearly cast models for these roles, and in terms of world-building, they should have cast plump women—the same women who supply milk would be the women who birth children.

Everyone in this film *does* something.

What's shocking is how shocking that is to see in a film in 2015.

Here's this movie saying "People aren't things" that *actually uses its camera work in a way that backs up its political position that people are not things.*

Perhaps that's the truly refreshing thing about this film, for me. It's that instead of women playing a part in some guy's story, in propping up some guy's journey, we have, instead, Max stumbling into Furiosa's story, and simply going along for the ride. He is, if anything, a Manic Pixie Dream Guy who stumbles in to suggest that she turn around and take the citadel herself. Then, after she has won the day and taken her rightful place as Queen Furiosa, he moves on to go help justice prevail somewhere else.

Max wins nothing for all his troubles. His only win is seeing a wrong made right.

A hero who does something because it's right, and reclaims his humanity, instead of doing it for a woman or loot reward! My god!

And in that moment, as I watched Max figuratively gallop off into the sunset, I realized that we've been missing those heroes. Those '80s loner dude heroes I loved were messed up, it's true—they were terrible at making connections with people. They were monstrous. But they used that monstrousness not for their own ends, but to help make the world just a little bit better. They were usually paired up with some more idealistic sort, a truer hero—a Furiosa. And they were doing actual penance for their inability to love. They expected nothing in return. Their names were not writ large. They didn't become kings. But the world was just a little better because they helped somebody else in a fight against injustice.

I love my gritty fantasy and SF stories. But I admit I'm getting tired of rooting for the bad guys who torture people and destroy buildings without a thought for those within. I'm ready to see conflicted nihilistic heroes who accidently get caught up in hope again, heroes who believe something can be saved, even if they must be dragged kicking and screaming into accepting their own humanity, out here in the light.

Tea, Bodies, and Business:
Remaking the Hero Archetype

HERO.

Okay, I want you to stop right there.

Think about what image popped into your mind when you read "hero." The first one.

NO CHEATING.

What's the *first* image your mind conjured on reading that word?

Hero.

Who is it?

Who is . . . *he?*

These days, when I read "hero" the image that pops up is some superhero, because I'm inundated with Marvel movie images all day. Thor comes to mind. Maybe, if I haven't been eating movies for a while, it's Conan.

Hero: a dude. Muscles. White. Butch.

Hero. First image. Every time.

It takes some additional thought, some retraining, for me to see anything but that archetype when I first think "hero." I have the same trouble with nearly every term we say is gender-neutral or totally inclusive that . . . well . . . turns out isn't. That's because when we learned what words meant, we had certain types of images placed in front of us. We learned to associate those images with the word.

We ate what the stories and media fed us, and it's why, to this day, we conjure them again and again when we see those words in text, when we hear them in conversations. We carry those expectations. It's why, often, we get so upset or simply surprised when the hero we see on the page doesn't conform to the image we learned.

Subverting expectations has become a hallmark of the gray, grimdark(er) fantasy tales now, and the even darker obsession in more general media with mythologizing serial killers (*Bates Motel*, *Hannibal*), elevating them to, if not heroes, then complex protagonists worthy of having their stories told; it's cultivating compassion for killers. Yet still, these antihero heroes are the same sorts of heroes: white, male, butch.

I can think of only two movies with women killers we're meant to sympathize with, and both because they'd been sexually assaulted—*Thelma and Louise* and *Monster*. And to be honest, I don't imagine anyone would call the women in these films heroes. The popular comic book mercenary Red Sonja is, perhaps, a proper hero, but is, once again, motivated by a sexual assault. Male heroes are heroic because of what's been done to women in their lives, often—the dead child, the dead wife. Women heroes are also heroic for what's been done to women . . . to them.

We build our heroes, too often, on terrible things done to women, instead of creating, simply, heroes who do things, who persevere in the face of overwhelming odds because it's the right thing to do.

It comes as little surprise, then, that though I'm known for writing gray, morally ambiguous antiheroes and heroes alike, I'm not asked to write about "heroes" in posts like these very often.

I am, more often, asked to write about "women heroes" or

"female heroes" and what makes those particularly gendered people special super unique from other heroes—and by "other," folks generally mean that first image, that initial burst of an archetype that comes to mind when we say "hero," and that means men. We mean the default hero. We mean the image our female heroes are being judged against instead of already standing alongside, popping up in our minds right next to our caped male heroes.

You may not catch the difference here, but I do, now. I hear it every time I'm asked to be on a panel about "strong female characters" or "women in science fiction." There's an implication when people ask, and the implication is that we aren't talking about women characters and women in science fiction or fantasy in the other panels, or in other spaces, or within other topics, so they—we—need to have our own special one, just to ensure we get five minutes where someone remembers women are heroes, and writers, and . . . *people*.

I want you to take a look at the title of this post again, and see what I did there. This post, I told you, was about heroes. Not women heroes, female heroes. But *heroes*. And it is.

The protagonist, Nyx, in my book *God's War* is a pretty standard antihero. I built her on the bones of Conan and Mad Max. She's everything I love about '80s action heroes, which includes sarcastic wit, endless persistence, an inability to commit, and the profound loyalty of those around her. I loved watching those heroes growing up—I loved reading about them in noir and science fiction thrillers. I just couldn't understand why they were all men. I couldn't understand why none of them could be women; I didn't know why the women were always sidekicks, plot hurdles, prizes, when I and all the women around me were heroes in our own lives. What were all these stories trying to say, collectively, about my ability to be heroic in my own life?

When Nyx sits down with a mark or an employer who offers

her tea, she doesn't drink it—she asks for a whisky. When people want to talk about the weather, or feelings, or the history of the world, she'll stop them. She wants to talk business. Bounties. Heads. She's a bounty hunter, and bodies are her business. This is her life. It's who she is. She's not some bit player in someone else's story. She *is* the story. She often ends the stories of others.

I built the societies in my new novel, *The Mirror Empire*, with a similar eye for heroic stories, for creating people, not archetypes, not the same old images many of us are fed as children. I worked hard to remember the other half of the world when I said "hero." Heroes all belong on the same slate, the same panel; they should all be here when we talk heroics, when we make strong protagonists. They don't need their own book, their own panel, their own post.

It turns out that I ended up with several soldiers, commanders, and generals in *The Mirror Empire* on top of my politicians, orphans, shepherds, and novice magic users, and I remember being concerned at one point, realizing one was the head of the militia in one country, another the war minister in a second country, and in a third country, I had a legion commander. Why such concern? I mean, after all, you see these characters in epic fantasies all the time. Books are stuffed full of them.

But in this particular case, when I wrote "head of the militia" and "war minister" and "legion commander," every single one of them was a female character. I had this irrational moment where I thought, "Oh no! I can't have so many women in positions of martial power. People will get them all confused."

Because if we're going to have a "strong female hero" there can only be one, right? One woman to prove the stereotypes. There's only one Smurfette.

Scrubbing that out of my brain took some doing. It took re-imagining my own vision of what types of people held these roles, and whether or not that was "okay." It turns out that when folks say "Why is character X a woman?" my response now is "Why not?"

Because there's no legitimate reason why not.

I will say that again: there is no legitimate reason the stories we create, the stories we read, cannot include a true representation of the makeup of the actual world around us.

I remember gender-swapping a character in *The Mirror Empire* at one point with much trepidation—I'd taken on the "Luke, I am your father!" trope and was trying to figure out how it was possible to play it as "Luke, I am your mother!" I had a mental resistance to it, like the Secret Parental Reveal somehow wouldn't work with a mother in the same way it would a father. But it turns out there was no good reason I couldn't—it's just that my expectation for this trope was, admittedly, based on Star Wars, and in Star Wars the reveal is about a father.

I was limited by stories that came before mine.

We are so often limited by our own expectations of stories, by the stories that came before, by the heroes who came before. . . . How is it we can bear to live with ourselves, as readers and storytellers, if we swallow those limitations without questioning them?

I like to challenge the expectations of story. I like to challenge the way I was taught language. I like to tear it down and remake it, because I see, so often, that what I was served up on a plate was, so often, in service to someone else's narrative, to someone else's wish for what the world would be—a world that did not include me, or people like me, a world that pretended we never existed at all.

That's not my world. And it's not the world I write about.

When our heroes are broken, it's up to us to remake them.

A Complexity of Desires:
Expectations of Sex and Sexuality
in Science Fiction

"OKAY," MY EDITOR WROTE IN THE MARGINS OF AN EARLY page in my first book, "we get it. She has sex with women and men."

Writing the character of Nyx—a bisexual bounty hunter with the brute sensibilities of Conan and grim optimism of a lottery junkie—was the first time I tackled writing a character who explicitly desired folks regardless of their sex. What she desired in folks tended to vary, but in general she found the too-pretty and the plainly ugly equally fascinating: the pretty because they seemed out of place on a toxic, contaminated world, and the ugly because it showed a degree of resilience; she liked to think she could see stories in their faces.

Communicating that should have been easy. I am, after all, not the straightest arrow in the quiver myself. But for some reason I found it necessary to make her desires really, really clear, and my clumsy authorial attempt stood out like a raised thumbprint on the page. LOOK HERE SEE THIS SHE LIKES DUDES AND GALS LOOK LOOK.

The reality was, I was writing with a straight white male gaze in mind. I was writing with the idea that her desire was somehow other, something that had to be explained to a reader who viewed straight as default. By pointing so loudly at her desire, I was automatically flagging it as something out of the ordinary.

But I was writing about a world that viewed bisexual and lesbian women as default, and that needed to come across in everything I wrote—from the way people non-react (and, in truth, expect) when women are married to women or have female lovers, to the way they talk about love and desire and sex. I had to rebuild the default narrative of "assume everyone's only attracted to people of the opposite biological sex" (and the assumption that intersex and trans folks don't exist) from the ground up.

Obviously, that expected default is a lie. It's always been a lie. But readers carry it. Writers carry it. Society carries it. Challenging it is a monumental task.

For starters, it meant rubbing out additional lines of narrative that *told* readers Nyx was bisexual, because to be honest, in this world there wasn't really a box like that. If strong female desire, and strong desire for other women, was the norm, it wouldn't need to be said. Think of it this way: if I had a man looking at a woman in a story and thinking about how much he'd like to go to bed with her, I wouldn't then say, "In Menscountry, it was natural for a man to desire a woman like this one. They may even go through a short courtship period leading to a monogamous marriage, a sort of commitment ceremony that often includes family and friends to witness the event."

No. I'd just note the attraction. End of story.

The cool thing about narrative is that the longer you're immersed in that narrative, the more normal it becomes for you as a writer (and, hopefully, as a reader). Because the society I'd built sent all its men off to war, the culture and its expectations had shifted. From a narrative standpoint, I wanted to build up a whole world where "woman" was default and women had automatic privilege, but do it in a way that felt organic to the story, while at the same time deconstructing ideas around default sexuality.

But, why did I care? Why did it matter so much, to me, to get this right?

In reading a great deal of science fiction growing up, perhaps I'd be forgiven for thinking that the most radical ideas of sex and sexuality around were Heinlein's strangely male-gazey polyamorous relationships (usually tending toward polygyny), people who had strangely hetero-seeming sex with aliens, and the occasional "tragic homosexual." If all I stuck with was that stuff, I'd think Nyx was revolutionary or some shit. And I'd have nobody to look to for help in making her world real.

But science fiction has changed a lot since the rollicking '50s, and I had a lot of other work to draw on in crafting a world with a different narrative. There was fascinating work in the latter half of the century from feminist science fiction writers in particular. I know everyone always quotes Le Guin here, but when I think of radical work, I think of folks like Joanna Russ, Naomi Mitchison, and Sam Delany. Later, Joan Slonczewski,[1] Gwyneth Jones, and even Storm Constantine, with many titles but in particular with *Wraeththu*, envisioned different ways human biology and conceptions behind default desire might change. And Nicola Griffith's *Ammonite* stands out as one of the first books I read published during my own adulthood that explored a fully female world.

Newer books, such as *Ascension* by Jacqueline Koyanagi and Malinda Lo's work in *Ash* and *Huntress*, rewrite old narratives (space opera and fairytales/mythology) that tell us what kinds of desire are normal, expected, or default. Jacqueline Carey skillfully challenges traditional attitudes toward sex in her Kushiel books, where the act of sex itself is considered holy, sacred, and taking pleasure in the erotic is likened to prayer. Elizabeth Bear touches on a range of relationships and desires in all of her work, but *Dust, Chill,* and *Grail* have always stood out for me in sheer variety.

The fascinating part about comparing newer SFF to the old is that, obviously, the desires of human beings themselves have not changed in a mere fifty years. But our ability to acknowledge, understand, and express them has been transformed by our cultural rewriting of the narrative around what's considered "normal" human sexuality.

When I speak to people about some of my concerns about how important stories are to the way we view our own lives and desires, and why words matter (even in posts on Reddit), I don't think a lot of people understand just how many regimes have sought to and succeeded in rewriting our past. In the United States, the 1950s was a time of great fear. We taught homogeny. We taught that anything outside a narrowly defined box was to be looked upon as suspect—a potential red terrorist threat. Our government, our schools, our media industry built a story about what was acceptable, normal, decent, and we all strove to fit neatly into it, though this story was completely made up. Is it any surprise that the narrative of the "caveman" going out to hunt meat for the tribe while the "cavewoman" stayed home and looked after the children became a staple of American history books during this time—a time when we also put forth the idea it was "normal" for men to go out to work while women stayed at home? (This was a narrative built in part to encourage women to get out of the workforce again so returning male veterans could fill their factory jobs.) I've been amused the last twenty years to watch the whole conception about how early hominids lived unraveled from its 1950s frame by more modern archaeologists.

Stories are powerfully important to people who are seeking to make sense of their own lives. Stories of what is possible open doors. Folks who snub their noses at the power of story must ask themselves why control over ideas—over books and media and information—is so coveted by governments. Why do totalitarian regimes destroy books? Why are people with radical ideas about how to organize other people put into prison?

The idea is the thing. The knowledge that things can be different.

The book that finally did it for me was Joanna Russ's *On Strike Against God*.

From the time I was small, I considered myself straight, always. I had an easy narrative. I liked to hang out with guys. There was never a question, really.

Until . . . well. Until. I fell hard for the girl in my college speech class when I was seventeen, a fiercely bright, boisterous young woman with a smile that could knock you flat. But when I felt it, when it hit me, I had no way to parse it. It was different than my draw to a guy, I told myself. Because when I spun out fantasies about spending time with her, it wasn't me, Kameron the woman, that she hung out with. It was me, Kameron the *guy*. Or, better yet, me transported into some other identity altogether—a guy named, oh, whatever, with some other life and a good job and easy laugh and great sense of humor. I'd have these long reveries about how, if I were a guy, I'd chat with her and ask her out and how much fun we'd have and how awesome I'd be and how we'd travel around the world together.

If only. If only I were a guy.

I couldn't conceive of a desire outside of a hetero one. All I saw, all I ate, was women desiring men. In books. In television. In movies. In fairytales. I knew that desire. I knew what to do with it. But this was different. Incomprehensible. I had no name for it. It existed in some fantastic realm where I was a dude.

Eventually I went off to college, and I'm sure she went on to have a very lovely life. But that fantasy would pop up sometimes. This fantasy of being a guy and therefore being suddenly free to woo the occasional woman I'd have a crush on. I honestly—dead serious—did not see this as "a lesbian thing." I had no story for it. No narrative. It was just something that sometimes happened. And it didn't happen often enough that it was a serious "issue" that I felt I needed to think about and interrogate. I had perfectly "hetero box normal" desire for men, which happened more often, and was so much easier to manage and deal with. No social stigma. No tricky, awkward conversations beyond the ones you'd see in bad romcoms. I could not actually imagine myself entering into a relationship with a woman, as a woman.

And then I read *On Strike Against God*, Joanna Russ's semiautobiographical book about coming to grips with her own sexuality. I was twenty-four by then, and thought I had my shit figured out. Russ talks about all the social constructs that enraged her about the marriage and children trap. She talks about being married. And then, later, she talks about this strange compulsion she has. . . .

She talks about how she's sitting in her car outside a bar and imagines flirting with one of the women there. In order to make it work, though, she imagines she's a man. She can't write the narrative of this desire any other way. It's too alien. She's never *seen* it before. And she realizes, in that moment, that it's not at all that she wants to be a man—she's quite comfortable in her female body. What she wants is the freedom to feel she can *act* on her impulse.

I sat there in bed and just stared at the page. I had never, ever, seen another person put into words this very strange occasional fantasy of mine, and name it for what it was—desire.

Stupid, right?

But when you are able to live comfortably within the hetero

box, it's easy not to question. It's easy to sweep strange compul-
sions under the rug. It's easy to pretend you're "normal," just like
everyone else.

But normal is a lie.

Normal is a story.

As a writer, it's my job to construct new normals for people.
It's my job to show folks what's possible. It's my job to rewrite
narratives. Because we can change these narratives. We can
choose better ones. We can tear it all down, and build it up again.
It makes us the most poorly paid but most powerful people in the
world. And I take that power seriously.

So when my editor wrote, "We get it. She has sex with women
and men," I crossed out the line of stupid narrative. Then went
back and got rid of some more. I made Nyx's world normal.

And by doing that, by crafting something different, I could
show people that maybe, just maybe, there were other ways to
be. Maybe not *this* way—Nyx is not the world's best person, and
her planet has some issues—but certainly people can live in *different* ways. We're all only as normal as the stories we tell ourselves.

What's So Scary about Strong Female Protagonists, Anyway?

THERE'S A WOMAN IN THE ALLEY YOU SHOULD BE AFRAID of, but you aren't, and you aren't sure why. You know her:

She is the woman on the cover of those urban fantasy novels. She's Buffy the Vampire Slayer. She's the woman on that show— you know, every show—who wears the tight leather pants and the bright lipstick and maybe she carries a gun or knows how to throw a punch.

But if you ran into her in an alley instead of a police station, you would most likely mistake her for a lost partygoer or perhaps a sex worker, and therein lies the real source of the trope she is meant to evoke to an assumed young male audience.

She is not meant to be scary, though she carries a gun and wears more leather than a man in a biker gang. She has tattoos, but not too many. She wears makeup, but not too much. She is neither too masculine nor too feminine. The coveted audience for much of our television programming remains the young (generally white) male, ages eighteen to thirty-four. It's why so many shows on the Syfy channel seem to want to find ways to disrobe their heroines for no good reason. And it's why the woman in the alley, the woman with the leather and tattoos (but not *too* many) is not actually scary. She is not meant to be any more dangerous than a carnival fun ride. She's meant to be a catalyst for an adventure, for a young man's sexual awakening—available, but not clingy. She is the woman you fuck, not the woman you marry.

It was not until I realized this that I understood why so many of the "strong female protagonists" I saw trotted out in many films and television shows and even a lot of fiction weren't the sort of strong female heroines *I* wanted to watch. These women were not created for me.

Worse, by parading this specific type of "strong woman" around as being the only type of "strong woman" there is, we're telling a generation of women that the only way to be taken seriously is to pick up a gun and get a tattoo. Guns and tattoos are fine things, but they are less a path to power than a head for mathematics and political reform. Our society may respect the stick, but it is the one who controls the person with the stick, not the person with the stick, who has the most power in our culture.

Yet there continues to be a proliferation of these women in much of the science fiction landscape—from books to film to television. The "post-Buffy" urban fantasy heroine has become a bit of a cliché, in no small part because the covers that portray her have all started to look alike. Hot pants, tattoos, over-the-shoulder glances; these are largely faceless heroines, women whose skin the assumed female reader can neatly slip into. They are witty and know how to use a weapon, but their "scariness" ends there. If the leather pants weren't a clue, the sexy poses should have tipped you off. These women are not meant to actually be threatening. Even if you're a vampire and she kills vampires, there's just as good a chance she'll sleep with you as shoot you. That's the conflict, after all.

But it's a conflict that isn't all that scary. It's just sexual tension wrapped up in another form. It's tough women as fetish, not as real people. The first time somebody wrote a Buffy rip-off was about as good as the first time somebody wrote a Tolkien rip-off, and then everything started to fall apart from there. It's not that there aren't plenty of good knock-offs, but at the end of the day, there are far more knock-offs than there are reimaginings. Or evolutions.

Unfortunately, once a marketing movement gets going, it becomes very difficult to kick your book out of it. I know one author who only tangentially included a fiery woman with a sword in their book, but lo, right there on the cover was a woman with a sword in skintight clothes in an over-the-shoulder pose.

I don't begrudge urban fantasy as a genre. It can certainly be a lot of fun for folks, though it's not generally my cup of tea. What bothers me about it is that it seems to reaffirm something I've suspected for a long time:

Women aren't allowed to be scary. Not *really* scary. Not in a nonsexualized, nonfetishized way.

Why is it all hot pants and back tattoos? Why the symbols of toughness instead of actual dark alley terror? Why do we celebrate "girl power" but sneer at "women power"?

I'd argue this is because women can be and are incredibly scary, and even if that's something powerful that we'd like to read about, we have to dress it up as something else. Something more relatable. Safer. Something that doesn't offend our loved ones and ensures that we are still loved and respected and not beaten up or harassed or made fun of for appreciating stories about women who can scare the crap out of the guy in the alley.

Urban fantasy is a great avenue for exploring women's real-world negotiations with power, but its heroines struggle with the same syrupy-sticky half-power that their real-world counterparts angst over. I want to be tough but lovable. I want to be cool but acceptable. I want power but not all the stigma that comes with power. I want to be special, but not so special that nobody loves me. I am equal, right, so why do I still feel like I have to be married or partnered or buried in children in order to be a real person? And if I'm so equal and so good at killing demons, why am I still making less money than guys? And if I'm so equal why do I still get terrified by every guy I see in a dark alley?

These are all great questions, and fun to explore, but they're not questions I'm interested in. I'm interested in what happens when women are no longer afraid of the guy in the alley. I'm interested in what happens if it's the *woman* in the alley who incites terror. Could that world exist? What would it look like? I want to unpack and reimagine what a truly free, powerful female heroine would look like. I want a Conan for women, who can chop up monsters and fearlessly bed whom she wishes without fear of repercussions or a dirty conscience. Who is she? What world does she live in?

And, most important of all . . . why don't we see more of her?

Are we just as afraid to write about her as we are to imagine her in that dark alley waiting, gun drawn, without pity or sympathy for man or beast or vampire or child, to blow off our head and hit the bar on the way home before slipping into blissful, dreamless sleep—the sleep of the unfettered, the conscienceless, the powerful? Her power, the real power, threatens our established social order. Women with real power can use it against men. Women with real power are not there to be looked at. They are there to act.

She is not the Strong Female Protagonist. She is the Scary Female Protagonist, and we don't see enough of her.

In Defense of Unlikable Women

"A FALL-DOWN DRUNK WHO'S TERRIBLE WITH RELATION-ships and makes some selfish, questionable choices goes in search of love, and fails at it."

This is actually the general plot to two films—the well-received, critically applauded film *Sideways*[1] and the much maligned, controversial film *Young Adult*.[2]

One follows a drunken, frumpy loser who steals money from his mother to enable his soon-to-be-married best friend to cheat on his soon-to-be-spouse; the other follows a drunken, frumpy loser who drives to small-town Minnesota to try to hook up with her happily married ex. Both films create stark, harrowing portraits of their protagonists' pathology and inability to connect to others. Both protagonists are even writers! The biggest difference in the reception of these films, I'd argue, is that one featured a male protagonist—and thus was critically celebrated. The other told the story of a deeply flawed woman, and became instantly "controversial" because of its "thoroughly unlikable" heroine.

I see this double standard pop up all the time in novels, too. We forgive our heroes even when they're drunken, aimless brutes or flawed noir figures who smoke too much and can't hold down

a steady relationship. In truth, we both sympathize with and celebrate these heroes; Conan is loved for his raw emotions, his gut
instincts, his tendency to solve problems through sheer force of
will. But the traits we love in many male heroes—their complexity, their confidence, their occasional bouts of selfish whim—
become, in female heroes, marks of the dreaded "unlikable
character."

Author Claire Messud takes this issue head-on in an interview
when her interviewer[3] says her female protagonist is unbearably
grim, and isn't Messud concerned that the protagonist isn't someone the reader wants to be friends with? Messud responds:

> For heaven's sake, what kind of question is that? Would you want
> to be friends with Humbert Humbert? Would you want to be
> friends with Mickey Sabbath? Saleem Sinai? Hamlet? Krapp?
> Oedipus? Oscar Wao? Antigone? Raskolnikov? Any of the char-
> acters in *The Corrections*? Any of the characters in *Infinite Jest*?
> Any of the characters in anything Pynchon has ever written? Or
> Martin Amis? Or Orhan Pamuk? Or Alice Munro, for that
> matter? If you're reading to find friends, you're in deep trouble.

Male writers, and their male protagonists, are expected to be
flawed and complex, but reader expectations for women writers
and their characters tend to be far more rigid. Women may stray,
but only so far. If they go on deep, alcoholic benders, they'd best
repent and sober up at the end. If they abandon their spouses and
children, they'd best end tragically, or make good. Women must,
above all, show kindness. Women may be strong—but they must
also, importantly, be vulnerable. If they are not, readers are more
likely to push back and label them unlikable.

I wrote an article[4] where I noted that in grad school, I sometimes drank two bottles of wine in a sitting and smoked ciga-

rettes. A couple of commenters on another forum said I must be an irresponsible alcoholic. I couldn't help wondering what their reaction would be on hearing a twenty-three-year-old male college student occasionally drank two bottles of wine in a sitting.

Boys will be boys, right? But women are alcoholics.

And so it goes.

But why is this? Why do we read the same behaviors so differently based on the presented sex of the person engaging in them?

I'd argue it's because women have been so often cast as mothers, potential mothers, caretakers, and servants, assistants, and handmaidens of all sorts that's it's become a conscious but also unconscious expectation that anyone who isn't—at least some of the time—must be inherently unnatural. And when we find a woman who doesn't fit this mold, we work hard to sweep her back into her box, because if she gets out, well . . . it might mean she has the ability to take on a multitude of roles.

Let's be real: if women were "naturally" anything, societies wouldn't spend so much time trying to police every aspect of their lives.

I like writing about complex people. I like writing about women. Hence, the women and men I write are flawed and complex. They have their own messed-up motivations. They don't always do the right thing. There's not generally a rousing ending where everyone realizes they were a jerk and has a big hug. Life is messier than that, and so are women. We're not any better or worse than anyone else. I'm flawed. I often make poor choices. I'm very often selfish.

So are many of the people I put on the page. And to be dead honest, I like them a whole lot better that way. Roxane Gay gives several examples of successfully unlikable heroines in fiction in her article "Not Here to Make Friends."[5] As Gay writes:

This is what is so rarely said about unlikable women in fiction—
that they aren't pretending, that they won't or can't pretend to
be someone they are not. They have neither the energy for it, nor
the desire. . . . Unlikable women refuse to give in to that temp-
tation. They are, instead, themselves. They accept the consequences of their choices and those consequences become stories
worth reading.

There is something hypnotic in unlikable male characters that
we don't allow in women, and it's this: we allow men to be confident, even arrogant, self-absorbed, narcissistic. But in our everyday lives, we do not hold up such women as leaders and role
models. We call them out as selfish harridans. They are wicked
stepmothers. Seeing these same women bashing their way through
the pages of our fiction elicits the same reaction. Women should
be nurturing. Their presence should be redeeming. Women
should know better.

Female heroes must act the part of the dutiful Wendy, while
male heroes get to be Peter Pan.

Pointing out this narrative, of course, isn't going to fix it. But
I do hope that it makes people more aware of it. When you find
yourself reading about a gun-slinging, whisky-drinking, Mad
Max apocalypse hero who you'd love if it was a guy but find pro-
foundly uncomfortable to read about when you learn it's a woman,
take a step back and ask why that is. Is it because this is truly a
person you can't empathize with, or because somebody told you
she was supposed to be back home playing mom to the Lost Boys,
not stabbing her landlord, stealing a motorcycle, and saving the
world?

Stories teach us empathy, and limiting the expression of humanity in our heroes entirely based on sex or gender does us all
a disservice. It places restrictions on what we consider human,

which dehumanizes the people we see who do not express traits that fit our narrow definition of what's acceptable.

Like it or not, failure of empathy in the face of unlikable women in fiction can often lead to a failure to empathize with women who don't follow all the rules in real life, too. I see this all the time in conversations with men and women alike. It's these same questions that get brought up when women who have been assaulted dare to report abuse. What was she wearing? Did she provoke him by talking back? Was she a bad wife? A bad girlfriend? Was she a good woman, or a bad woman? This line of questioning, and the assumptions that prompt it, is one we would never apply to their male counterparts—unless they are men of color. Was he wearing shorts when he was robbed? Did he yell at his neighbor before he was shot? Did he smoke pot at any time in his life before he was shot by a police officer in the street? Was he a good man, or a bad man?

This justification of violence against those who step outside of the roles the dominant culture puts them into can be reinforced or challenged by the stories we tell. Stories tell us not only who we are, but who we can be. They paint the narrow behavioral boxes within which we put ourselves and those we know. They can encourage compassion and kindness and acceptance, or violence and intolerance and reprisal. It all bleeds from the page or the screen into the real world. Who deserves forgiveness? I'd hope we all do.

Women and Gentlemen:
On Unmasking the Sobering Reality
of Hyper-Masculine Characters

IN THE MOVIE *THE JEWEL OF THE NILE*, SEQUEL TO *Romancing the Stone*, romance author Joan Wilder has written herself into a corner. Pirates have boarded the ship containing her heroine and the heroine's lover. First, Wilder writes that the hero sacrifices himself to the pirates, allowing the heroine to get away in a rowboat—women and children first, after all.

But Wilder finds herself deeply unsatisfied with this turn of events. It's pretty cliché, after all, and this was 1985—women's lib, all that. So she rewrites it so the heroine sacrifices herself to allow her lover to get away. Stuck now with her heroine in the hands of the pirates and her formerly swashbuckling hero cowering in a rowboat, Wilder, frustrated with her choices, throws her typewriter overboard.

Whatever option she chose, it all felt ridiculous. After almost twenty years writing fiction, it's an impulse I can sympathize with.

When I started writing short fiction, I spent a lot of time writing sword-and-sorceress stories. I wrote about women who wielded swords and magic, who sacrificed themselves for greater causes, whose concerns were lovers and children. If I flipped them

from women to men, they would be considered, perhaps, softer
sorts of heroes—goody-goodies, a little too warm, a little too
self-sacrificing. For boys, anyway.

Odd, I thought, that I would read these characters differently
with a gender reversal. Why was that?

There was something that bugged me about how I wrote these
women. It was like I put a sword in her hand and it didn't change
her. It's like I didn't consider how a life of violence would transform a person. I didn't consider how training a person to kill, and
putting them in violent situations, would badly damage the way
they interacted with the rest of the world outside a battlefield.

Like Wilder, I felt like I was writing my characters into situations that simply weren't satisfying.

I had a deep love of '80s postapocalypse movies and science
fiction classics. Lone-gun hero types with no attachments, incapable of forming long-term relationships, valorized for their
ability to bust down walls and shoot bad guys, but often incapable of living in civilized society. I looked at these male action
heroes and wondered if we would cheer and celebrate them,
their antisocial behavior wholly unquestioned, just as loudly if
they were women.

So I began to write about the sort of heroes I loved—whisky-
drinking, gun-toting, lone-wolf types—and I made them women.

At first, I thought this was going to be really fun. I'd have these
swashbuckling, heroic women who didn't care about anyone or
anything, forging off to do battle. And yeah, for the most part,
it was fun. But then something interesting started to happen.

By turning squads of soldiers committing war crimes into
women in my short story "Wonder Maul Doll,"[1] and invading
forces from other shores into women in "The Women of Our
Occupation,"[2] I started to peel back the "normalcy" we attach to
this extreme sort of masculinity and uncover the rottenness at

much of its core—while simultaneously creating more interesting and complex visions of women.

In my novel *God's War*, I created a former government assassin turned bounty hunter who was also a war vet. She could accomplish some insane acts of violence. She was notoriously tough to kill. But becoming a killing machine had taken its toll. For all the blood and glory, achieving this pinnacle of strength and perfection her society encouraged required her to give up being able to function within any kind of settled civilization. She couldn't have normal relationships. She struggled to have friends. She self-medicated with whisky and mild narcotics. She found the idea of motherhood suspect at best.

I had, I realized, created a monster.

I'd created an '80s action hero.

By putting women into these hyper-masculine roles, I was simultaneously challenging the portrayal of women in fiction as the people who have things done to them (as opposed to the people who *do* things) and encouraging readers to take another look at both the benefits and severe drawbacks of that type of masculinity.

We toss men into the maw of war and call them weak or shell-shocked or mad for coming back physically changed. We say a man who hits women and children is a bully and a coward, but call him weak for expressing emotions beyond anger and rage. Putting my female characters into this masculinity trap, where they were expected to perform violence and shut down emotion, gave me a new view of the expectations we have of many men in this society, expectations that linger in the broader media even as we, as individuals, cry out for change.

Expectations of masculinity can creep up on you, because to some extent we still view "masculine" as normal, the default, and "feminine" behavior as "other." If you think this is not the case, see what happens when you send your son to school in a dress. We can pretend all we like that women are equal, but as long as men and women are continually encouraged to suppress the broad aspects of their humanity that we decry as "feminine," we're all screwed.

Because it's those things we celebrate as "other" that make us truly human. It's what we label "soft" or "feminine" that makes civilization possible. It's our empathy, our ability to care and nurture and connect. It's our ability to come together. To build. To remake. Asking men to cut away their "feminine" traits asks them to cut away half their humanity, just as asking women to suppress their "masculine" traits asks them to deny their full autonomy.

What makes us human is not one or the other—the fist or the open palm—it's our ability to embrace both, and choose the appropriate action for the situation we're in. Because to deny one half—to burn down the world or refuse to defend the world from those who would burn it—is to deny our humanity and become something less than human.

When I see other writers[3] celebrating their masculine stories in worlds that are 90 percent male, I wonder, often, if they've forgotten the full humanity of the people they're writing about. If they fail to see and interrogate what happens when they erase half an individual, and half the world, they're suffering an incredible failure of imagination. A willful blindness. It's celebrating a broken world that never was.

I, too, grew up on Conan stories and Mad Max. I grew up celebrating dangerous alpha males who fucked and drank and blew shit up with no consequences. But whereas other authors, perhaps, grew up to emulate this writing and construct these hypermasculine heroes without question, I started to think about how Conan would actually get along in a world. I started to think about ways that hyper-masculinity would affect the quality of characters' lives. I realized that Conan would never have a happy ending. Whether or not that's something to celebrate, I don't know. But it's something we should talk about.

What I found when I started to explore the full potential of my characters was that my stories got better, too. I wasn't impeding the possibilities of my characters with lazy stereotypes, expected conflicts, and failures of imagination. I was looking at all the different ways we express our humanity.

I was writing about people. Not caricatures.

When we go forward to forge new worlds—fantastic, science fictional—we could do worse than remember that just as our worlds are constructed, the people within them are constructed, too. We create boxes and toss people into them, regardless of their intrinsic ability to fight or nurture or build or destroy. How your characters navigate those social expectations and responsibilities has less to do with their physical sex than it does with the ways they choose to adhere to or fight those expectations.

So maybe it's your hero who gets the rowboat, or your heroine. Or maybe, in truth, there's another option—maybe they turn and fight the pirates together. Maybe they skillfully talk them out of plunder with a witty, well-chosen story or clever ruse. Maybe there's another way out. Maybe it's not either/or.

That's the far more interesting story—what our characters do when they're allowed to be people, not parodies of our own flawed expectations.

Gender, Family, Nookie:
The Speculative Frontier

SOMEONE ONCE ASKED ME WHY "ALPHA MALES" WERE SO popular in so much romantic speculative fiction, and I hesitated to answer it. Not because I didn't know, but because I knew I was going to have to have a discussion about teasing out the difference between finding pleasure in something you genuinely find pleasurable and taking pleasure in something you think you're supposed to find pleasurable. This is a tough question for anyone who's taken it up—do you truly delight in displaying certain types of behavior, or in the display of certain behaviors by others, or are you just taught you're supposed to like it, so you convince yourself it's great?

We live in a culture that controls people through a grim hierarchy. Anyone who's ever been bullied in school knows exactly what it looks like, and how it seeks to keep us in our places; the folks at the top work to establish dominance and power. They are the ones who succeed, because the game is rigged in their favor. When you add onto that hierarchy the place of women in it, when it was only about fifty years ago when women couldn't buy a house or get a credit card without their husbands' permission, it makes sense for women to make alliances with men who are bullies. Men who are bullies can protect women from other men who target them. The bully who is known to you is far less scary than the one who is not. Fetishizing that behavior when your choices are limited is not surprising.

Funny enough, this tolerance for bullies breaks down the more egalitarian a society is—one need only look up the hilarious exploits of pickup artists trying to neg women in Amsterdam and Canada to find that this fetishization of the bully doesn't hold as the hierarchy breaks down. Yet when I see my colleagues writing far-future fiction, or secondary-world fiction, the fetishization of the bully comes with them, even on worlds they may have rewritten as egalitarian. But why? Well, because that's how the story is told. That's what we expect.

That's what we keep writing.

I was watching an old '80s movie last week called *Broadcast News*. It's about this go-getter television producer who has a thing for an empty-headed, good-looking newscaster and about a ho-hum-looking but very smart reporter who's been her best friend for ages. I loved the heroine to pieces—her job comes first, she tries to leap into bed with the good-looking newscaster on first meeting him (he gently turns her down), and she packs condoms in her purse. (What happened to these '80s heroines? Where are they in media today?) It was, I thought, a standard romcom, and I went into it expecting a standard romcom resolution. After all—the television producer must choose one of these guys, right? But as the movie progressed, I found myself increasingly disturbed at the idea that she'd end up with either of them. Neither was a good fit. The good-looking one was just too empty-headed for her, and didn't have her journalistic ethics. And the supposed "good guy" displayed a serious mean streak on being rejected that made it clear he was one of those pseudo "nice guys" who's only nice until you tell him once and for all you won't sleep with him. So imagine my surprise when (spoilers!) we get to the end of the movie and she does, in fact, choose *neither*. She takes a big promotion and we fast forward into the future, where they're all living successful lives, all friends again, and she's been dating some other person a few months. It reminded me of the relief I felt at Buffy being able to walk away without a date at the end of the series.

But the expectations I brought to the film were romcom expectations: This is how the formula works. This is how these humans will work. Like human beings and relationships are puzzle boxes with only one solvable formula. In fact, life is far more complicated than that, but we don't always want to see that in our fiction. We want to believe it's all quite simple.

From a reader's perspective, simplicity is great. But from a writer's perspective—especially one writing at the limits of the imagination—the way that science fiction and fantasy novelists create futures that look just like our assumptions about how the world operates today isn't simplicity—it's laziness.

Even our nonfiction perpetuates this idea that the way we are today is the way we've always been, or will ever be. I recently saw my first few episodes of *Cosmos*, a show I probably would have interrogated less before I started untangling the stories we tell ourselves are history. As with every other depiction of "early humans," this one showed a recognizable, to us, family group: women holding children, a couple men out hunting, maybe a grandma off to one side. They looked like the limited family groups we know from popular media instead of the likely far more complicated ones that early humans moved in during their time: four women and two men stripping a carcass, two men out gathering, an old man watching after the children, two old women tending the fire. The truth is that every archaeologist and historian is limited by their own present in interpreting the past. So when

Americans and Europeans talk about early humans, they don't talk so much about early humans in Africa, even if that's where we all came from. When we talk about early humans, they're always hairy, pelt-wearing pale folks hacking out a living on some ice sheet. The men are always out hunting (like good 1950s office workers!), while women stay in camp to dandle babies on their knees. In fact, small family groups like these could not afford truly specialized roles until the advent of agriculture. Before that, folks needed to work together even more closely to survive—every member pulled their weight, whether that was looking after young children, gathering food, or herding some big mammal off a cliff and stripping it for meat.[1]

One of the best ways of keeping people in line is telling them that certain behavior is "normal" and "has always been done that way." I'll often hear parents lament about how difficult it is to raise young children, and say they feel like failures because they must go out into the world and make money, and be good parents, and be good partners, while living on month after month, year after year, of sleep deprivation. In truth, the advent of the two-parent household is a fairly modern invention—extended families have generally been the norm throughout history, with multiple generations often living under one roof. No one in their right mind would set up a system where just two adults were around to mind the crazy schedules of infants. What these stories of the past, and of "normal," do is tell us it's just us that's broken, not the social structures we've created in service to an 8 to 5 office or factory life.

Yet I still see this construction of families falling down in much of the fiction I read, let alone the often far more conservative media I ingest via movies and television. It wasn't so long ago when doing something like portraying the life of a happy single mother was tut-tutted by executives and producers, and an interracial family was considered taboo on the screen. But novels and stories are often bound by fewer constraints. We have less pressing overlords. So the only thing that keeps us from portraying new and different ways of social behavior is simply the limit of our own imaginations, and our willingness to buy into the common narrative of family structures, of gender binary, of conventional procreative sex.

Everyone writes science fiction and fantasy for different reasons. I get that. But I'm not here to write it to tell people the same old stories. I'm not here to comfort folks who've chosen to live and organize themselves in certain ways and say, "Yes, of course. It's always been this way. It will only ever be this way." I'm here to make worlds that are really different. I'm here to challenge assumptions of normal, of hierarchy, assumptions that humans will always be bullies, or assumptions that "man" and "woman" are anything but poorly constructed language boxes created by humans to organize what is, in truth, a fantastically messy and diverse and incredibly nonbinary world.

I write about consent cultures. Matriarchies. Third genders. I write about futures at war, and at peace. Futures powered by bugs, or star magic, or ThunderCats. If I'm writing about the limits of things, then I must step out of the narrow narrative boxes of broader media and many of my colleagues and seek out stuff that pushes at that, poking at it with a stick until it all comes undone. I read widely, and build on the work from the fringes that came before me—work like Geoff Ryman's *The Warrior Who Carried Life*, Candas Jane Dorsey's *Black Wine*, Samuel Delany's *Trouble on Triton*, Joanna Russ's "When It Changed," and new work by folks like Jacqueline Koyanagi, Ann Leckie, and Benjanun Sriduangkaew that challenges what we consider "normal" human relationships and gendered ways of being.

The way we challenge convention—the pushing out of the

margins—very often happens first in fiction, and bleeds out from that media into larger fandoms, from comics to film to television, and I'm pleased to be part of the massive push for expanding our imaginations and busting down the limitations we place on our own lives.

Story is powerful. It can hold us back. Box us in. But it can also challenge our assumptions. Teach us to build structures. Or tear down those structures altogether and start over again anew.

Anything is possible. But to make it possible, we must first acknowledge that none of it is normal.

The Increasingly Poor Economics of Penning Problematic Stories

MY SPOUSE HAS BEEN TRYING TO GET ME TO PLAY *SPACE Run* for a while. It's cute little game where you build your own spaceship and take it on missions. I played through the tutorial recently, only a little annoyed that I wasn't able to choose a female gendered character. The tutorial was okay. I moved on to taking the first mission, which is given to you, the protagonist, by a female CEO. After getting the mission, my heroic avatar felt the need to comment to his android sidekick about how "hot" the quest giver was.

I turned off the game.

The reality was, I had plenty of other games to play—*Portal, Skyrim, Monument Valley, The Room*, and replays of *Mass Effect 3* and *Dragon Age: Origins*—not to mention books to read like *City of Stairs, Shield and Crocus, Hild*, and *Steles of the Sky*, that were better entertainment and not annoying sexist face-punchy.

It was in this moment that I realized the true economics of what's going to drive the storytelling change. See, it used to be the only media you could consume was the racist, sexist, homophobic sort. That was simply all there was. So you either ate it, grimacing the whole while, or you opted out of it. (I opted out of comics. I read pretty much no comics until the last six or seven years, as finding things that weren't punching me in the face was hard.) But these days? Well, there's a *lot* of media out there, a lot of entertainment, and there are, increasingly, more diverse stories and choices we can make.

It's gotten to the point where I'll actually ask before I choose a film if it's got any sexual assault or threats of same before I decide to watch it. When I'm annoyed, stressed, and exhausted, I don't want to spend what should be entertaining downtime gritting my teeth through uncomfortable microaggressions aimed at women. I get enough of that all day in real life. I want some fucking escapism. And if there are films that can give me that, I'm going to prefer those over the ones that don't.

Many say that it's the shifting demographics of the United States that will force many media companies to make changes—by 2050, 50 percent of the United States will be made up of people of color. But women have always been 50 percent of the United States . . . so why haven't we seen more media treating us like humans? It didn't occur to me until I turned off *Space Run* in annoyance that what's also going to change things up is that media itself has opened up. Just about anyone can create a game and put it online. Anyone can write a book and post it on a retail platform. We've got far more opportunities for choice now, and though big Hollywood studios and publishers are still releasing primarily status-quo stuff, they're changing, too. What they see is that when presented with more choices, less problematic choices, people are quite often choosing them over their messy, face-punching bullshit.

The funniest part about my experience with *Space Run* is that it wasn't even egregious. I've gotten through far worse things—*True Detective*,[1] *BioShock Infinite*—that I endured because there were other aspects of the storytelling that were so good. But when you give me a mediocre experience and *then* punch me in the face, well, you know . . . fuck it. This is why I'll put up with *Guardians of the Galaxy* having a weirdly womanizing hero and its sole female protagonist being called a whore, because it offers, at least, other things that I enjoy. I will still, of course, call out this problematic behavior, but, you know, if the rest of the movie were *also* shit, I wouldn't bother with my dollars. What studios will start to understand, though, is that if I am given an equally good romp of a show that has more heroines, none of which are called whores, and an actual nice-guy hero who doesn't confuse women with paper towels one minute and act like a human with feelings the next, I'll choose that over the more problematic *Guardians of the Galaxy*[2] anytime.

Freeing up the story platforms—video, publishing, gaming—so that more people can play has indeed given us a glut of shit. But it's given us a glut of choice, too, and we can choose media that doesn't insult us a lot more easily now than before. It's not just the same bullshit on the same four television stations. I can root out stories like *Orphan Black* and even *Snowpiercer* among the dreck, and turn off the stuff that annoys me. I can find other stories. As a creator, I can actively write other stories, and deliver them to people, more easily too. And increasingly, I find that though I considered what I was writing to be stuff on the margins, it is actually pushing in a bit toward . . . well . . . if not mainstream, then at least carving out its own niche with audiences like me who are actively turning off bullshit stuff because they know there's more interesting work out there.

We can rant all we want about how it's hard to find the good stuff in the bullshit—but opening up those floodgates has also made it possible for the storytelling narrative to diversify and shift. I like more choices. I like being able to choose better stories, instead of being forced to endure the shitty ones or go without.

✖

Postscript: A year or so after I wrote this, *Jurassic World*, with its gender-reductive mishmash of terrible Indiana Jones–lite, career-woman-who-should-be-a-mother tropes, came out and *grossed half a billion dollars* its opening weekend. But my faith in humanity was, of course, restored when *Star Wars: The Force Awakens*—with its female protagonist and nonwhite male leads— dominated even the dinosaurs at the box office, shattering all prior records. There's hope for us all yet.

Making People Care:
Storytelling in Fiction vs. Marketing

I'M GOING TO TELL YOU A STORY.

It's how I began my most popular essay to date, "We Have Always Fought," which went on to win a Hugo Award for Best Related Work, get nominated for a British Fantasy Award for Best Nonfiction, be reprinted twice, and be translated into many languages.

You might think there's no correlation between how I began that essay and its success, but I'd challenge that assertion. The truth is that "We Have Always Fought" doesn't say anything particularly new and mind-blowing about the role of women in combat throughout history. Take a women's history course or pick up some books or spend more than a passing moment Googling the issue and you'll come to some of the same conclusions. We have women combat veterans. They exist. They have always existed. But we don't see them. We don't talk about them. We don't write enough stories about them.

And when we stop telling stories about people, we forget them. We erase them from the collective history of our lives, our cultures.

All I did was tell a story.

I write about a book a year while holding down a day job writing marketing and advertising copy. Folks ask me, often, if the marketing work steals a lot of creative energy for fiction. But the truth is that they're different types of writing. In fiction, I'm the only real stakeholder. People can give me a lot of suggestions, but I don't have to take any of them. In marketing, I'm usually the person at the very bottom of the decision hierarchy. Folks come to me for words and ideas and then run off with them, often to the extent that I don't recognize the final product. To be sure, some projects are more successful than others, and a great ad project is a true team effort, with everybody bringing their best ideas, and clients acknowledging they did indeed come to you for those, instead of plastering over what you bring them with their own vision.

What's this have to do with story? Hold on. We're getting there.

One of the big things these two types of work have in common is that my goal in both is to make people care about something—in both cases you might see it as a product, whether I'm selling a book or toilet bowl cleaner. In the case of the book, though, what we aim to get people invested in is the characters. When folks are emotionally invested in a story, they're far more likely to gush about it to others. And if they're not in love with your characters, you'd better have an astonishingly compelling story. The story, the "what if," keeps people turning pages even when they're not in love.

It's the same in some types of advertising. If I can't get you to form an emotional connection to a place, a product—Disney, Coke, and McDonald's are masters of emotional manipulation like this—then what I want to do is tell a story so compelling that you can't look away. Brands like to sponsor athletes and tell stories of overcoming adversity so that you'll associate the strength of the athlete's body or resolve (or both) with their product. It's the sort of magical thinking that says, "Drink PowerAde and you'll be a great athlete too!"

Storytelling is how we've passed on social mores, history, and morality in our cultures for tens of thousands of years. Storytelling is a universal: every culture does it. There's a reason our religious books aren't simply a list of shall-and-shall-nots. Morals and teachings are contained in stories, which are studied, dissected and passed down; we *remember* stories in a way we don't remember lists of facts.

Storytelling instead of info dumping is a fairly well-known life hack,[1] but there are still very few people who tell stories instead of facts. Even in marketing circles, where this is our business and we should deploy stories ruthlessly, I still get direction from stakeholders who want facts and bullet points. I hear exclamations about how the folks we're talking to are analytical. But an analytical person is not an emotionless robot.

In life, as in business, it's much easier for us to fall back on the safety of "logic." If we're just logical enough, reasoned enough, we'll sway people to our side. But people are not swayed by logic. People use logic to back up their emotional decisions.

I could tell you that over and over again, or I could tell you this story:

At my day job, we'd been trying to sell a software upgrade to a pool of existing users for some time without much success. Our response rates were approaching zero. One of the things the marketing manager told me was that people adored this product; they were steadfast fans, but they were so attached to the current version that no one could see any good reason to upgrade. They'd already sent piece after piece of bulleted, logical items about all the benefits of upgrading, and how much better the product was, and offered discounts. It didn't work.

While floating ideas with my creative director I said, "What if we send a love letter from the product? Like, nothing creepy, but something like 'We've had a lot of great times together in the past, and I've been working to improve myself so that we can work even better together'?"

We managed to get the marketing manager on board (I'm still stunned) mainly because nothing else was working. The designer and creative director designed a really nice envelope with classy heart-shaped cutouts and signed it off "XOXO." I framed the copy as if this was coming from a beloved, trusted partner who had been improving just for the users. We included a discount offer on the upgrade as an added carrot.

The day after the mailer went out, the responses started to roll in. The first was from a customer who said to their software rep, "I want to use my *love* coupon!"

Yeah, they were pretty into it.

We went from barely measurable responses to industry standard responses overnight, all because we found a way to tell a story that connected with people on an emotional level instead of a logical one. The truth is we *want* to fall in love. We *want* to care. Even when we know the game.

This works broadly across a variety of audiences, and it's something I think a lot about when crafting marketing pieces. I still bump into resistance a lot—I write more bullet-pointed emails than you can imagine—but the pieces that make people care, that make people feel, that evoke an emotional reaction are the pieces that last. That's how you create a customer for life, instead of just grabbing a quick sale from somebody price-hunting.

It turns out that novels are much the same way. People share books that they love. We find ourselves, as writers, trying to figure out what "sells" books. And the reality is that what sells books is writing something people love so much, and are so connected to or titillated by or excited by that they want to tell their friends, so they can discuss it endlessly, write fanfic about it, draw the characters, cosplay as the characters, get tattoos of symbols or people in the book, and celebrate the next release in the series as if it were a holiday. It's love that sells books, not bullet points.

What readers or customers love, however, is not always easy to deduce. Sometimes it's merely a trick of luck, of happenstance, where your work taps into the current cultural zeitgeist. Right time, right place.

But at the heart of every story is our desire for an emotional connection and catharsis. I've sat in creative meetings about software products where we aren't talking about product screens and buzzwords, but about customers freed from the desktop computers at their auto dealerships who can keep track of business from their smart watch at their kid's baseball game. "Never miss another game—or another deal." We don't sell things. We sell the emotion, the experience, that that thing gives us.

And when I write an essay, I'm not selling you on treating people better. I'm not berating you, or giving facts and statistics. I'm telling you a story about llamas, and how we write about them, and how writing about them changes them, and us, in ways we never expected.

"I'm going to tell you a story."

The story is who we are. The story is how we change the world.

What's your story?

Our Dystopia: Imagining More Hopeful Futures

IF YOU CAME OF AGE IN THE 1950S AND '60S YOU WERE promised a future of world peace and flying cars, so I can understand being a little disappointed with what we've ended up with. But if I hear one more person pine after a flying car I'll tell them they should have built it. The utopia of flying cars and space colonies isn't the future we've built. I came of age reading science fiction after 1980. I was promised a cyberpunk dystopia ruled by corporations, complete with violent reality TV and authoritarian governments, and well—here we are. I was rewatching the original *Total Recall* movie recently—with its security body scanners and self-driving cabs and terrorist battles—and couldn't help admiring how well this future mirrored my reality. We may not be on Mars, but the ubiquitous evil corporations and invasive technology sure are here.

We can get angry about the fact that this is the future we've built or acknowledge that if this was what we chose to build, we're fully capable of creating something else. Want a Star Trek future of world peace and slinky jumpsuits? We can do that, too. If you can dream it, you can make. It goes for dystopias and utopias alike.

Science fiction writers create all sorts of futures—that comes with the job. But it's not the type that matters—hopeful or dark— it's the variety we see as readers. It's nurturing the imaginations of those who will go on to create the world around us. Not just the technology but also the social policies, attitudes toward natural resources, the realities of climate change, even our ever-evolving sense of morality.

When I was in my early twenties I watched *The Man Who Fell to Earth* with David Bowie because I'd heard so much about it, and I admit that I didn't get it. My girlfriend at the time looked up some chatter about the film and said it was supposed to be a metaphor for how life grinds you down. Bowie is a Martian come to Earth to save his family, but as the years pass and his plans to save them wither on the vine with every bureaucratic roadblock, he eventually gives up. He turns to drink and whimsy. His people are dead. Why should he care anymore?

It's this resignation with getting a future we didn't want that the people in charge are relying on. The systems are too old, too ingrained. Power cannot be moved. These structures have always been here. This is the only way the future can be.

They love it when we think this.

Yet, like so much of the world we're told about, it's all a lie. It doesn't really exist. The future is malleable. That's what they don't want you to know.

When you believe people can't change the world, they win.

Of course people can change the world. Who do you think got us here in the first place?

We did not talk much about a malleable future when I was a kid. Mostly my dad was obsessed with the idea that we would get AIDS. It was the scariest part of the future he could see for his daughters, and he gave us lectures about girls who had sex once and got AIDS and died of it. It was sex as a death sentence. The future as death. Maybe this is why I'm so hopeful about the future: the one I could see coming in the middle of the '80s, with AIDS deaths climbing and the fear of a Cold War apocalypse and rising crime and rioting countries and the images of Somalia's famine, all looked like dispatches from a future that would go on and on just like this: a future of death and violence and nuclear disaster.

I guess our cyberpunk, corporation-ruled future isn't so bad when you look at what most folks at the time thought we were in for. At least a cyberpunk future is a future. Not a fiery end.

So in a sense, we really did get the most hopeful future we wrote.

People often ask me about the power and purpose of science fiction. Are we future-prophets? Should there be a religion founded on William Gibson texts? Should we make Octavia Butler our patron saint of change? Will Connie Willis found the next Scientology spin-off?

I don't think we're seers. Most of us can't even predict what we'll have for lunch tomorrow. I'm even conflicted about the idea of us on advisory committees for NASA. We don't know the future any better than anyone else. If you'd asked me in 1988, I'd certainly have thought the world would have exploded into a fiery World War Three by now and we would all be being hunted by Terminator robots. In truth, some of the worlds I created, like the one in my God's War trilogy, look far more like post-apocalypse novels than anything else. That's still the future I turn my head toward when shit gets real. It's the future I know. It's the one I grew up with.

* * *

When I consider building more hopeful futures, I actually wonder if that's the right idea. Maybe it's the terrifying apocalypse books that helped us avoid nuclear meltdown. Maybe it's fear of pandemics that ensures the CDC gets any decent funding at all. Maybe we are nurturing just the right amount of fear to keep us avoiding disaster.

I would argue that it's a mix of fear and hope that sustains us. It's reading *A Canticle for Leibowitz*, which posits a future where we all blow ourselves to hell several times, and then watching a few episodes of *Star Trek* to balance it out. It's believing it's possible to get our shit together, while admitting that it may not be anytime soon. It's saying we're staring into the edge of the apocalypse, but we may be able to stave it off just a little bit longer.

So when people ask me, Where are the hopeful futures? I say, I'm writing some of those too, but they have to live alongside the terrible ones, the fearful ones, the nuclear holocaust we narrowly avoided, the AIDS epidemic that went from death sentence to chronic illness. We need them to exist together because if we forget the worst case, we can't appreciate what we have, and if we don't have the more hopeful ending, we won't know to strive for that. We won't even know it's possible.

These are the stories we must have, this balance of light and dark, hope and fear. It is the two sides of our nature given voice. It's acknowledging a future of many possibilities and allowing them to coexist in a way that we will never experience in real life. This is the power and promise of science fiction, this magic of creating and living in every possible future. It's a power I love to pieces. It's a power that comes with a terrible responsibility, to ensure that we avoid the worst that we are capable of while continually striving to transform into the best that humanity is possible of becoming.

Where Have All the Women Gone?
Reclaiming the Future of Fiction

"WOMEN DON'T WRITE EPIC FANTASY."

If I had a dollar for every time some dude on Reddit said something that started with "Women don't . . .", I'd be so rich I wouldn't be reading Reddit.

Erasure of the past doesn't always follow a grand purge or sweeping gesture. There's no great legislative movement or concerted group of arsonists torching houses to bury evidence (that's usually done to inspire terror). No, erasure of the past happens slowly and often quietly, by degrees.

In her book *How to Suppress Women's Writing*, science fiction writer Joanna Russ wrote the first internet misogyny bingo card—in 1983. She listed the most common ways that women's writing—and, more broadly, their accomplishments and contributions to society—were dismissed and ultimately erased in conversation. They were:

1. She didn't write it.

The easiest, and oftentimes the first appearing in conversation, is the simple "women don't" or "women didn't." If delivered to an indifferent or ignorant audience, this is often where the conversation stops, especially if the person speaking is a man given some measure of authority. "Women never went to war" or "Women simply aren't great artists" or "Women never invented anything" are common utterances so ridiculous that to refute them becomes tedious. As I grow older, I've ceased making long lists of women who, in fact, *did*. More often, I'll reply with the more succinct, "You're full of shit. Stop talking." If, however, the person who says this is challenged with evidence that yes, in fact, women have and women do, and here are the examples and the lists, the conversational misogyny bingo moves on to . . .

2. She wrote it, but she shouldn't have.

I hear this one about my own writing a lot, and I see it applied to romance writers and other outspoken feminists in particular. The writing is too sexual, too political, too feminist, or even— funny enough—too masculine to be *real* writing. This type of writing, because it is written by women, is considered somehow deviant or disorderly. It puts me in mind of those angered at the idea that science fiction is only good if it isn't "political," which is code for "does not reinforce or adhere to the worldview shaped by my personal political beliefs." The reality is that all work is political. Work that reinforces the status quo is just as political as work that challenges it. But somehow this type of work is considered particularly abhorrent when it's written by women.

3. She wrote it, but look what she wrote about.

Men, famously, can write about anything and be taken seriously. Jonathan Franzen writes books about family squabbles. Nicholas Sparks writes romance novels. Yet these same subjects, when written by women, are assumed to be of lesser note; unimportant. Jennifer Weiner is especially vocal about this erasure of the weight of her own work. Yes, she wrote it, they will say, but of course she wrote about romance, about family, about the kitchen, about the bedroom, and because we see those as feminized spheres, women's stories about them are dismissed. There is no rational reason for this, of course, just as there's no rational reason for any of this erasure. One would think that books by women written about traditionally women's spaces would win tons of awards, as women would be the assumed experts in this area, but as Nicola Griffith's recent study of the gender breakdown of major awards shows, women writing about women still win fewer awards, reviews, and recognition than men writing about . . . anything.[1]

Writers of color also see this one in spades—yes, they wrote it, but it wasn't about white people's experiences. Toni Morrison labored for a very long time to finally get the recognition her work deserved. It took a concerted effort, complete with very public protest, to finally get her a National Book Award. Arguments were made that Morrison's work was dismissed because she wrote about the experiences of black people. This type of erasure and dismissal based on who is writing about whom is rampant. While white writers are praised for writing about nonwhite experiences, and men are praised for writing about women, anyone else writing about the experiences of the people and experiences they know intimately is rubbed out.

4. She wrote it, but she wrote only one of it.

Few creators make just one of anything, including writers. It generally takes a few tries to get to that "one-hit" book, if one ever achieves it. We also tend to remember writers for a single, seminal text, as with Susanna Clarke's massive undertaking, *Jonathan Strange and Mr. Norrell*. Yet Clarke also has a short story collection available—though few hear about it. Others, like Frank Herbert, write a number of wonderful novels but become known for just one great text, like *Dune*. Few would argue that Herbert only wrote one novel worth remembering, but I have checked this off on the bingo card listening to someone dismiss Ursula Le Guin because "she really only wrote one great book and that was *The Left Hand of Darkness*." A lack of reading breadth and depth is on the reader, not the author. But one sees this applied most often to women writers. "Yes, that was a great book, but she only wrote one book, so how great or important could she really be?" one says, forgetting her twelve other books.

5. She wrote it, but she isn't really an artist, and it isn't really art.

Genre writers have contended with this one for years—men and women alike— but this excuse for dismissal is still more often used against women. Even within the genres, women's work is skewered more often as being not "really" fantasy, or science fiction, or simply not "serious" for one reason or another. It's a "women's book" or a "romance book" or "some fantasy book with a talking horse for God's sake" (I actually saw a female writer's book dismissed this way after it showed up on the Arthur C. Clarke Award shortlist one year, as if whale-shaped aliens and time travel were any less ridiculous).

Women's backgrounds are also combed over more than men's, especially in geek circles, and you see this with the "fake geek girl" backlash, too. Is she a *real* engineer? Okay, but did she actually work for NASA or just *consult* for them? "Yes, she wrote a science fiction book, but it doesn't have real science in it" or "Yes, she wrote a science fiction book but it's about people, not science" are popular ways of dismissing women's work as being not "really" part of the genres they are written in, or simply not real, serious art the way that those stories by men about aliens who can totally breed with humans are.

6. *She wrote it, but she had help.*

I see this one most with women who have husbands or partners who are also writers. Women whose fathers are writers also struggle with this dismissal. Rhianna Pratchett, a successful writer in her own right, finds her work constantly compared to her father Terry's, and, coincidently, folks always seem to find ways her work isn't as "good," though Rhianna's style and her father's are completely different. For centuries, women who did manage to put out work, like Mary Shelley, were assumed to have simply come up with ideas that their more famous male partners and spouses wrote for them. The question "So, who *really* writes your books?" is one that women writers still often get today.

7. *She wrote it, but she's an anomaly.*

The "singular woman" problem is . . . a problem. We often call this the "Smurfette principle." This means that there's only allowed to be one woman in a story with male heroes. You see this in superhero movies (there is Black Widow and . . . yeah, that's it). You see it in cartoons (April, in *Teenage Mutant Ninja Turtles*). And you see it in awards and "best of" lists, typically but not always written by men, who will list nine books by men and one book by a woman, and that woman is generally Ursula Le Guin, Robin Hobb, or Lois Bujold. The singular woman expectation means that when we do see more than one woman in a group, or on a list, we think we've reached parity. Studies have shown that when women make up just 30 percent of a group, men and women alike believe there are an equal number of men and women in the room. At 50 percent women—a figure we see so little in media representation that it appears anomalous—we believe that women outnumber men in the group. What this means is that every woman writer is given an impossible task— she must strive to be "the one" or be erased.

When we start to list more than one female scientist ("Yes, there was Marie Curie" tends to be the answer when one asks about women scientists), or astronaut, or race car driver, or politician, we're often accused of weighting women's contributions more heavily than men's. Though my essay "We Have Always Fought," about the roles of women in combat, was largely well received, most criticism of the piece rested on this accusation: that by focusing on remembering and acknowledging the roles of women in combat, I was somehow erasing or diminishing the roles of men. "Yes, women fought," the (largely male) commenters would admit, "but they were anomalies."

8. She wrote it BUT . . .

The experiences I write about in my fantasy and science fiction novels tend to be very grim. My work comes out of the tradition of both new weird—a combination of creeping horror and fantastical world-building—and grimdark, a label most often applied to gritty, "realistic" fantasy that focuses on the grim realities of combat and a nihilistic "everything is awful" worldview. Yet when my work hit the shelves I was amused to see many people insist my work was neither new weird nor grimdark. There was too much science fiction, or not enough sexual assault against women (!) or too much magic (?) or some other "but." Watching my own work kicked out of categories I was specifically writing within was a real lesson in "She wrote it but . . ." And lest you think categories don't matter, remember this: categories are how we shelve and remember work in our memory. If we're unable to give those books a frame of reference, we are less likely to recall them when asked.

I am still more likely to find my work remembered when people ask, "Who are your favorite women writers?" than "Who are your favorite science fiction writers?"

And that, there, demonstrates how categorization and erasure happen in our back brains without our conscious understanding of what it is we're doing. Yes, I'm a writer, but . . .

When you start looking at reactions to the work of some of your favorite women writers, you will see these excuses for why her work is not canon, or not spoken about, or not given awards, or not reviewed. I could read a comment section in a review of a woman's work, or a post about how sexism suppresses the cultural memory of women's work, and check off all of them.

The question becomes, once we are aware of these common ways to dismiss women's work, how do we go about combating them? These ways of disregarding our work have gone on for centuries, and have become so commonplace that men are used to deploying them without challenge as a means to end all debate.

I'd argue that the easiest way to change a behavior is first to become aware of it. Watch for it. Understand it for what it is. And then you *must* call it out. I've taken to typing "Bingo!" in comments sections when these arguments roll out, and linking to Russ's list. When we see sexist and racist behavior, the only way to change that is to point it out and make it clear that it's not okay. The reason people continue to engage in certain types of behaviors is because they receive positive feedback from peers, and no one challenges them on their assertions. If we stop swallowing these excuses, and nodding along when people use them, we take away the positive reinforcement and lack of pushback that's made it possible for them to use these methods of dismissal.

Because I write such dark stories, many people think that I'm a pessimistic person. But that's not true. I'm a grim optimist. I understand that the road to a better future is long and bitter and often feels hopeless. Yes, there is a warm gooey core of hope I carry with me at the very center of myself, and it is the hope of someone who knows that change is difficult, and feels impossible, but that even a history that has suppressed and erased so much cannot cover up the fact that change is possible.

LET'S GET PERSONAL

Finding Hope in Tragedy:
Why I Read Dark Fiction

IN 2006, I WOKE UP IN THE ICU, BLOOD POURING DOWN one arm from a line the doctor was desperately trying to get in my arm. He was down on one knee, like he was going to propose, my arm flung out in front of him.

"I'm sorry," he said, "I'm sorry. I'm sorry."

He kept saying it. Over and over. My girlfriend stood next to me, gripping my hand. I was in intense pain, but even so, I couldn't understand why he kept apologizing. My brain was a muddled gray mush, but I understood this much:

The pain was necessary. Expected.

They needed to get a line in me, you see, because I was dying.

And I knew it.

I read a lot of dark books. I'm a fan of the weird, the creepy, the strange. I have a fondness for Jeff VanderMeer and K. J. Bishop and Angela Carter. I read H. P. Lovecraft only until it started to give me active nightmares. I've read everything by Christopher Priest, including the certainly not-at-all-upbeat *Fugue for a Darkening Island*. I devoured Melvin Burgess's *Bloodtide* and *Bloodsong* like milky honey.

As a teen, I had people try to get me to read Terry Pratchett and Piers Anthony, but it just never took. I was getting something out of dark fiction, some catharsis, that I wasn't getting from other books with lots of laughs or tidy, upbeat endings.

"How can you read all that stuff?" people would ask me.

Life is fucking depressing enough.

I'm learning how to hot-wire a car. Or, rather, start one without a key. It's twenty below zero and it has been dark since 3:30 p.m. I'm huddled in a van that technically isn't stolen but technically doesn't belong to either me or my buddy. The owner admitted herself to a local institution after trying to kill herself, and supposedly, my friend says, handed him the keys so he could have access to the car. But he lost the keys. So we've busted open the panel covering the steering column and taken out the metal ignition cover. It turns out hot-wiring an old van like this is actually pretty easy, because there aren't any hot wires involved. You just bust open the steering column and use any old key to turn the broken ignition switch.

Voila.

Of course, it also means you can't lock the car. So it's a good thing we're college kids with nothing worth stealing.

A group of us pile into the van and race out into the middle of some fucking field, not far from campus but, you know—in Fairbanks, Alaska, you don't need to go far to find yourself in the middle of nothing.

The northern lights are out. A lot of people are drunk.

I hang out the side of the van, wind in my face.

I've never felt so alive.

* * *

The truth is, life can be painful. It can be a horror. When I got laid off from my job in Chicago, six months after the ICU trip, I didn't have any savings. No safety net. Because of U.S. health insurance laws at the time, I had to continue paying for health insurance or risk becoming uninsurable even under an employer plan. Health insurance then, without a job, cost me $800 a month and didn't actually pay for a dime of the $500 a month that my new medication cost.

Chronic illness is a fucking piece of shit, like getting hammered upside the head with a fucking shovel. They tell me it's an immune disorder, and there's nothing I could have done to prevent it. So sorry for you. Too bad. Could be worse. There are worse illnesses.

I started trying to stretch out my medication doses to last longer than they were supposed to. In no time at all, I was living on expired medication whose efficacy was constantly in question. Would today be a good day, or would I pass out somewhere?

Death had never felt so close.

Life is fucking dark, sometimes.

The trouble is, when you're pressed facefirst into shit, all you can think about is trying to stay alive. It's all you do, when you're really desperate—you try to live. There's no time to emote, no time to figure it out, no time to sit on the bed and cry and feel sorry for yourself. When you're faced with your own problems—real, tangible, I-could-fucking-die problems—you have to deal with them.

But a fictional problem?

Somebody else is dealing with that. You're just along for the ride.

It means you get to spend the whole ride actually feeling things, instead of buttoning it all the fuck back up so you can live.

This is the story of my life: getting called a monster because I do instead of feel, because I act instead of emote.

My week back at the house after the ICU visit, I saw blood every time I closed my eyes. My arms were filled with needle marks, covered in bruises. The pain was so bad, and I was so weak, I couldn't even prepare my own meals—I didn't have the strength to wield a knife.

I'd lost a tremendous amount of weight the last year, and more in the ICU. It was like I lived in someone else's body. I felt disconnected.

At night, I'd lie in bed, and when I closed my eyes I'd jerk awake again, haunted by sounds and smells and that blood—that blood gushing from my arm, pooling on the floor. I could smell the hospital antiseptic.

My week in the hospital, I was hooked up with a catheter. They took my blood every three hours. At one point I had an orderly throw a wet towel at me and tell me to wash myself. My period started. The catheter leaked. I spent a day lying in my own blood and urine.

It came back every time I closed my eyes.

But I couldn't process what had happened to me. I had thousands of dollars in medical bills. Rent had to be paid. I had to get back to work. I didn't have enough PTO time to miss work. I had to get back to work. Had to get back to living.

Gotta go. Gotta move.

I pretended I wasn't broken, because if I let myself be broken, I wasn't going to make it.

* * *

I'm not actually sure when I started writing dark fiction. I know I started writing *God's War* the year I was dying. I was losing a lot of weight and drinking a lot of water, but nobody could figure out what was wrong with me.

It certainly started out as a dark little book; a war-weary world, a world-weary protagonist. But after I got back from the hospital, after I started measuring out my life in medication, something changed.

Because I realized something then, looking at all the medical bullshit keeping me alive:

Every life is a tragedy.

We are all going to die.

There is no other ending, no matter the choices you make.

My first hospital visit after getting out of the ICU, I walked into the hospital bathroom and had a panic attack.

It was the strangest thing. One minute, I'm totally fine. I'm cool and collected. I'm just seeing my doctor, to deal with this bullshit illness.

But when I went into the bathroom and washed my hands, I smelled it: the antiseptic soap.

I'd first smelled it in the ICU, during that bloody horror show of a week.

I started to shake.

I went back into the bathroom stall and sat down. I burst into tears.

No reason.

Just the smell. The panic.

I'd been a body on a slab; a thing, subhuman.

Wash yourself.

* * *

I just finished playing a game called *Mass Effect 3*, the third in the Mass Effect franchise, naturally. It has a really contentious ending. The galaxy is being destroyed by an evil alien force.

It's clear from the opening scene that you're basically fucked. No matter what you choose, you're fucked.

I knew this from the very start. Right from the opening. I saw what was coming. I saw we were all fucked. And I played that game faster than any game I've ever played, because I could feel the urgency—yes, we're all fucked, but we're going to save the galaxy. I'm going to get there. I'm going to save it.

It's a relentlessly dark game, but it's just a game, right?

Yet I found myself playing this game and crying the whole way through it. I cried through the whole ending, because I knew. I knew from the very beginning. I knew how it would end.

We're all going to die.

But it was different, when I played the game. When I played it through in the game, it wasn't like in real life, when I had to keep moving, I had to keep sucking air; gotta find a job, figure out how to pay insurance bills, pack up my shit, move to a new place. . . .

When I played the game, it was the character taking all these hits. It was the character who was letting people down. It was the character who had to keep moving.

And that freed me up to actually feel something.

I could actually roll through all those terrible emotions—the broken despair, the horror, the fear, the rage, the sorrow. I didn't have to muscle through. I could spend forty hours of game time emoting, and not feel bad about it.

When I got to the end of the game, it was perfect, for me.

Because I knew from the start we were all going to die.

The challenge was having the fortitude to keep going when you knew you were going to die, when you knew it was all going to end.

For the character. For the fake galaxy.
For me, eventually.
And all of us.

I'm not sure where I picked up this relentless way of muscling through things without stopping to process them. I think it's a survival thing. My mom does this too, during times of great stress. The whole world bleeds away, and I get this laser focus. It means I'm incredibly good during times of fear and panic and crazy, but it can be days or weeks before I actually bust down and process what happened.

Reading tragedies, I realized, connecting with characters who persevered in the face of grim odds and certain ends . . . was actually comfort reading for me.

All you have to decide, as they say, is what you do with the time given.

Public Speaking While Fat

MY BODY HAS ALWAYS BEEN A PLACE OF BATTLE.
When I was younger, it was personal, self-inflicted strife encouraged by schoolyard taunts of "water buffalo!" and "pig!" supplemented by family matriarchs who were permanently obsessed with the width of their own asses (and, very often, mine and that of my siblings) despite advanced degrees, working-class jobs that soon became high-powered ones, and increasing awards and honors.

Near-death helped me put my body project into perspective. Three or four hours of exercise a day to maintain a still pleasantly plump physique seemed overkill. Hating myself when death had been so close, now that I had a chronic illness, seemed the worst sort of irony. So I gave up hating myself. It was weirdly liberating.

But giving up on one's self-inflicted angst does not magically erase the pressures of a society that hems you in from all sides.

I admit that looking at pictures of myself the last couple of years always involves a bit of dissonance. Since my first novel came out and I switched to a job that no longer requires me to bike into work every day, I have—as has happened to many writers—put on about seventy pounds. This is easy to forget when you work at home a lot and don't go out much. There are perfectly good reasons for this gain, as my metabolism is super-efficient; I come from a long line of overweight people with a host of immune disorders who could, however, survive famines quite well. Folks often ask me how I can hold down a day job, freelance, and write a book a year. The answer is quite simple: I roll out of bed and I write. I am sitting in bed, right before I go to sleep, and I am typing away. My life has become a constant war with deadlines, trying to maintain momentum during book releases.

I've worked at hacking the fitness of this—I'm writing this article right now from the comfort of my treadmill desk—but the hard-core two hours a day I used to do is just something I'm not able to do and still write the 1500 to 3000 words of fiction-related work and associated blog posts I do every day. I hope to find that balance eventually, but the last few years have been hard.

The funny thing that people don't get when they see me living it up at writing conventions is that I have, in fact, always been considered fat. From the time I was five years old, people told me I was fat. I was a size 14 in high school, and people told me I was fat. I was working out two hours a day when *God's War* came out, eschewing ALL THE CARBS, and at 220 pounds, I was, of course, fat. And the thing is, when you're fat at 220 pounds, you're still fat at 290 pounds. There's not a whole lot of societal difference. You maybe get hit on a little more at 220 than at 290, but that's about it.

I have done a lot of broken things trying to get back to that 220, including calorie counting, which ended disastrously. I lost twenty-five pounds, sure, but the minute I stopped, I gained it all back plus thirty pounds, which is what's put me over the edge with those airplane seats; my time at the treadmill desk and indoor bike desk is all about fighting to keep me under the weight at which I can no longer fly. I knew better than to calorie count like that, but was feeling the societal pressure to punch back down a size. That was a mistake.

When people come to me about fears of public speaking while fat, about heckling, about online harassment, I feel it necessary to remind people that I got the same amount of harassment for being "fat" at 220 as I do for being "fat" at 290. As a woman, *you are always going to be fat*. People are always going to trot that one out to try to insult you, like taking up more space in the world, as a woman, is the absolute worst thing you can do.

Which I, of course, find hilarious.

And yet, I get it. I do. I feel it.

As internet bandwidth has increased, we've entered the age of the quick video, the vlogger, the YouTube sensation, the Skype session. I've felt an increased pressure, as a writer, to not only go out in public but to widely share my public image in ways that are often beyond my control.

I've been asked more and more to complete video projects, not just for fiction endeavors—acceptance speeches, video blogs, Google hangouts, taped panels, and the like—but also for job interviews. Yes, really. I realized, with increasing unease, that being both female and fat were two huge strikes against me in any video medium, no matter what I thought of myself. I was going to have to be twenty times as brilliant with a waggling chin than my male counterparts. Because as much as I didn't hate myself, and was happy to toss a couple years' worth of body project hours into actual, tangible accomplishments the way a dude would, it wasn't my immediate accomplishments

I was going to get judged on by casual observers. I'd be judged on whether or not I had the "discipline" to take up less space in the world.

Immediately. On sight. Snap judgment.

There's a reason I keep photos off all my books. I've been well aware since birth that, as a woman, if your appearance does nothing to advance your cause, best not to flaunt it.

When I was in high school, there was a brief period where I flirted with the idea of giving up writing to pursue acting full-time, because I was pretty decent at it. I still pull on my theater training to accomplish extroverted events. But I quickly understood that if you're heavier or taller than the male lead, your chances of being chosen to star across from him are incredibly small, no matter how rockin' your talent. Only severe illness and near-death got me to a "normal" weight in Chicago. To get within ten pounds of that in Alaska, I spent three hours a day at the gym, six days a week, and lived on eggs, rice, mixed veggies, and string cheese. For a college kid who found school very easy, giving over this much time and headspace to a body project was a chore, sure, but not impossible. I could look more or less "normal" by dedicating my entire life, from waking to sleeping, to acting supremely abnormally.

Obsessing over a body project left me less time for real work. For writing. For speaking. For activism.

As, I suspect, is intended by this societal obsession, spending time dedicated to the body meant less time dedicated to being an actual politically powerful member of said society.

I was talking to a feminist writer/reviewer at a science fiction convention who said she was actually reading my blog back in the early days when it was called *Brutal Women*, and she'd found it via the guest posts I did at *Big Fat Blog*, which I participated in very, very early in my online life. I have always considered fear and hatred of taking up space as a feminist issue, as it's so often used to shame women, no matter what their actual size.

Having gained and lost the same eighty pounds three times in the last fifteen years, I can honestly say I'm familiar with that cycle of fear and shame. The only time I've ever been praised for my weight repeatedly was when I was dying. I'll never forget my mother on the phone with my dad, having just gotten me out of the ICU, telling him how great I looked because I was so thin, and, you know . . . something broke in me after that comment. When I pulled on my size 12 pants and they were loose, something I'd not experienced since fifth grade, all the feels washed over me—how fake this all was, how our success was measured in the width of our asses, how my worth went up only as I lay dying.

I vowed from that moment on, crying in my too-big pants, that I would never, ever beat myself up or hate myself for being fat ever again.

And I haven't.

But it doesn't mean I don't think about it sometimes, and it doesn't mean I don't occasionally feel anxiety about public events, and I don't occasionally wince at pictures and feel a moment of dissonance—after all, we're not used to seeing fat people represented positively in media, and my brain wants to rebel. But that fear and hate, that internalized fat shaming and body hatred I had growing up—I've learned to reject that outright as bad programming.

Doing this—fucking the programming—is really freeing. It means I can stand up at a reading and give a performance in a loud, snarky voice. It means I can sit on and moderate panels without fear. Because I know how fat shaming works. I know that if somebody wanted to try to shame me using the "fat" callout, the same person would say that no matter what my weight.

I can change all I want, trying to contort my body in all sorts of ways, but those people, our society, will stay the same. They will always, always try to burn you down with some half-baked call of "cunt" or "fat" or "insert female-gendered slur here." And just like the fact that I have a cunt is not likely to change, the fact that I take up a lot of space in the world—no matter the range on that massive sliding scale—is not going to change either, unless I'm dying. And I'm sorry, my friends, but I have no intention of dying so people can sit around saying how "good" I look. Fuck you.

So for folks who fear having a large voice, especially those of us who've grown up with bad programming, I can say this: just like with everything else, yes, you will have to be smarter, and work harder. But don't let societal bullshit keep you down. It's made to stop you from speaking. It's made to get you to shut up, and stay home, and take up less space in spaces men consider "theirs."

When you view it that way, when you see it for what it is, it becomes a bit easier to step up and step out, because you realize that in some small way, you going out into the world when it wants to shut you up is, itself, an act of resistance.

Many women-identified people worry about heckling, about people pointing and shouting, "You're fat! You're not a real woman! You're stupid! You talk too much!" and I get that the pain and fear and sorrow over that can be too much. But being in these spaces, and being heard in them, is vitally important to changing these conversations, to challenging the narratives about our worth and what we say and what we think that have been created by others.

Go forth into the world, retreat when it is too much, but

know that when you stand up to be heard and be counted, you're doing your own part to change the narrative, and in doing so, to change the world. I promise I'll be standing there next to you.

They'll Come for You . . . Whether You Speak Up or Not

DURING TIMES OF GREAT SOCIAL UPHEAVAL, IT CAN OFTEN seem safer to say nothing. You get noticed less. You piss off fewer people. You just make sure the trains run on time. You make your dollars and go home and stuff them in the mattress and keep your head down and hope they don't come for you.

It's a silly position, really, because they *always* come for you.

I think it's easier to remain neutral on stuff like politics when you think that specific policies won't affect you. If you aren't a woman, or nonwhite, or gay, or disabled, or poor, or chronically ill, it's really easy to just keep your head down and shut up. "It's not my concern," you say, while totally forgetting that we live in a world where our own quality of life is directly impacted by the quality of life of others (vaccinations are a really easy one to point to; so's universal health care). We forget that our way of life— access to life-saving drugs, clean water, abundance of food—is wholly contingent on the skills and abilities of many millions of others who support the systems that care for us. We also forget that for many of us, being a part of some of these groups harshly affected by social policies is just one accident or "bad luck" incident away. Poverty, chronic illness, and disability can happen gradually or suddenly, often when you're paying the least attention.

I say all this as somebody who grew up upholding '80s action-movie masculinity as the pinnacle of cool. I always liked the idea that strong people were loners who pulled themselves up by their own bootstraps, who had witty lines and impeccable health and virility and nobody messed with them. This was more about who I wanted to be than who I wanted to date, mind, and it really influenced how I viewed other people. Life sucks? Do something about it. Stop whining. Nobody keeps you down but yourself.

I'm still gung-ho about assertiveness, negotiating for yourself, standing up to injustice, and the like, but I'm far less likely to tell people that all they should be doing is looking out for themselves, and fuck everybody else. When you look at the way we've constructed our entire society, very few of us would thrive in a place where we had to be totally self-sufficient. Illness would kill a great many of us, and childbirth, accidents, starvation . . . We rely on other people to help us succeed, however invisible those millions of hands are as we pick up that orange at the grocery store or pop a pill to help prevent heart disease or drive a gas-powered car forty miles to work across a publicly funded road.

I didn't have a real appreciation for just how much we rely on other people until my pancreas blew out when I was twenty-six. Immune disorder, they told me. Sorry. Now you have to take five to six shots a day just to survive. The only reason I live is because there are people creating synthetic insulin in a lab.

That whole independent '80s apocalypse hero I'd hoped to style myself after kind of imploded along with my pancreas, because even if I raided every pharmacy from here to the ocean after the End Times, it's all got a one-year expiration date. If modern society implodes, I do too, no matter how tough, smart, and savvy I am.

It gives you a lot of perspective, being at the edge of death all the time. I've gotten really touchy with doctors, health insurance providers, and pharmacies. I scream and yell at them a lot, because when you need something to survive, it makes you a tad nutty if it looks like you may not be able to get it.

It has humbled me a lot, and given me a great deal of empathy.

Being a woman certainly also has disadvantages in our society, but for much of my life, until I really entered the workforce, I could pretend I was a guy, you know, a "real person" and not one of those femmy women that everyone made fun of like they were useless. It wasn't until I went out into the real world, among strangers far removed from my cozy hometown, that I realized there were people who looked at me as prey just for being a woman, and people who assumed I cared about things, or did things, or wanted things completely based on my gender instead of what I could do. I got passed up for a raise at the movie the-ater I worked at because managers had to learn to run the pro-jection booth, and the reels were seventy pounds. Nobody ever asked me if I could lift seventy pounds (of course I can). They just assumed I couldn't. So I wasn't even considered. (I learned this later. Things changed, and some women marshaled through by being overly insistent, but it never occurred to me that I'd have to *fight* for something I was obviously qualified for. I still thought I was a white guy, after all.)

That was the first time I realized that I was going to be at a disadvantage in the workplace, and that I was going to have to work just a little bit harder than everybody else to get noticed just as much. I had a lot of advantages, too, but I learned early that I had to telegraph them.

I'll never forget the time my parents went to a swanky restaurant with us kids and received terrible service. We weren't exactly dressed like royalty, and my mom told me that we'd likely been dissed because we looked poor, and the server assumed we'd leave a bad tip. Knowing that we would return the next night and it was likely we'd get the same server, my parents left a huge tip. I thought this bit of reverse psychology was a roiling pile of shit. But the next night, lo and behold, we got the same server, and boy whoa howdy was he nice to us. "As long as people think you have money," my parents told me, "they will treat you really well."

"Having money" or clout or any other type of invisible advantage will always be invisible in your first interaction unless you like to go everywhere dressed like a celebrity. So, like my parents did, you have to telegraph it quickly in every new interaction. People will see you first as a woman, or nonwhite, or a poor person, or if you go there holding hands with a same-sex date, as a gay person, and you'll have to fight for every inch of respect you get from them.

I could pretend that legislation regarding women's reproductive choices, or health care in general, don't affect me. I could pretend that it doesn't matter whether or not we think nonwhite people or queer people are, you know, actual *people*. When it comes to being queer, I'm invisible, being married to a guy, and when it comes to being nonwhite, well, I'm white, so who cares, right? But all I have to do is think about what it's like when people make assumptions about *me* based on shitty movies and crap TV shows and outrageous, ingrained cultural assumptions about women, or queer people, or people with a chronic illness, and then I realize I'm fucked. I'm one of the ones they're coming for.

When people talk about why we shouldn't have universal health care because poor people don't deserve to be alive, I remind myself that the people who say that are just one health catastrophe away from changing their minds. But it helps if some of us remind them of that.

It takes a good many people to keep me alive. I recognize that I need to take steps to support them, too, because we're nothing without each other. That's a position I could shut up about, or tuck under a rug, for fear of, I don't know, angry emails or lost book sales, but let's be honest here—the people who think women and nonwhite people aren't human are probably the least likely to pick up a book with first lines like mine anyway.

I spent a great deal of my life trying to be quiet and nice and not piss anyone off. I was miserable. It served no purpose. And they still came for me. It made me even easier to dismiss, to overlook, to assume I was just somebody else everybody could roll over and spout off ridiculously sexist, racist crap to without dissent.

But nodding and smiling gets old. It makes it easier for people to box you up and ship you off. I'm only really alive when I'm pissing people off anyway.

The Horror Novel You'll Never Have to Live: Surviving Without Health Insurance

THERE WAS A TIME BEFORE THE AFFORDABLE CARE ACT. Before health insurance was subsidized by the government, and before we were all guaranteed coverage no matter our medical conditions. I grew up in that time, and it nearly destroyed me.

In 2005, I was a robust twenty-five-year-old living in Chicago and working as a project assistant for an architectural and engineering firm. In the fall of 2005, I started to lose weight.

This was a good thing, I figured. I worked out a lot. I ate right. It's just that losing weight got . . . easier. It was nice. After so many years of working out relentlessly just to stay at a reasonable size, I didn't have to think about my weight anymore. As the months passed, I experienced other problems, though. I started to get recurring yeast infections—infections that could only be cured with prescription medications, not the usual over-the-counter stuff. My gums bled when I brushed my teeth. Not just a little blood, but bloody spitfuls of the stuff. I was thirsty all the time, to the point where I could barely survive a forty-five-minute plane ride to Indianapolis without having at least one tea or juice on hand. I honest to God thought I was going to die if I couldn't have a large drink every hour. And when I got ingrown hairs, they would form huge pustules on my body that had to be lanced and drained. As the months passed, the symptoms got worse. My sinus infections dragged on and on. When I went to various urgent care doctors and explained that I was exhausted all the time and getting weird infections, they said I must just be stressed out.

I was so tired, in fact, that I couldn't get out of bed on time for work. I started to get confused, and had trouble concentrating. My boss had to call me in twice for making data entry errors that I hadn't had problems with before. I dragged my ass into work an hour late sometimes. An hour late! But I was so exhausted and frazzled I didn't care; nothing seemed to really matter except sleeping and drinking juice. I also became increasingly hungry in addition to thirsty. I had to eat an extra meal between breakfast and lunch. I was chowing down on burgers and ice cream for lunch . . . and continuing to lose weight.

I remember lying in the bathtub and rolling up into a sitting position and feeling the bones of my spine against the tub. It hurt. I didn't have the usual padding there to protect me from the hard tub. It was like being inside someone else's body. I had a "catastrophic" health insurance plan through my employer, so when I went to the doctor with these complaints, it was always to somewhere cheap like the twenty-four-hour urgent care or Planned Parenthood. I had a $2500 deductible, so everything was out of pocket. I was twenty-five years old, making $40,000 a year living in Chicago; after rent and paying my student loans, it didn't occur to me to spend a bunch of money on tests. I was twenty-five! Surely there wasn't anything wrong with me but stress. I never went to the same doctor, so there was nobody to connect the dots related to my various symptoms.

My body finally gave out one Friday after coming home from Indianapolis for a work-related trip. I stepped off the train and got myself a hot dog because I was so hungry. But it gave me such bad heartburn I had to stop eating it. I trundled home via the bus. I could barely walk up the three flights of stairs to my apartment. I was so goddamn tired. I came home and drank and drank and drank—water and juice and Gatorade. And I peed and peed and peed. It was all I could do to stumble from my bed to the bathroom. I had to grab hold of the couch for balance.

At some point, my roommate and girlfriend at the time found me standing in the bathroom. Just . . . standing there staring at the door. She brought me to the couch, where I apparently went into convulsions and started vomiting. I blacked out and wasn't fully conscious for thirty-six to forty-eight hours, when I woke up in the ICU and had a doctor patiently explain to me that I had type 1 diabetes, an immune disorder that usually shows up in children, which is why nobody thought to test me for it at twenty-five. Sometime the year before, an immune response from my body had backfired, and my immune system started killing the islet cells in my pancreas that produce insulin. I would no longer be able to survive without taking four to five shots of synthetic insulin a day and carefully measuring and monitoring everything I ate and all of my physical activity.

What they did not tell me was that having this immune disorder also meant that outside of an employer-sponsored health insurance plan, I was now forever uninsurable. And the medication it took to keep me alive was going to cost me $500 to $800 a month without insurance. The ICU trip alone was over $20,000, with thousands more in bills coming in for weeks and weeks after I got out of the hospital. Even after my $2500 deductible, I still owed 20 percent of that cost. That was with insurance. I just laughed at these bills. Laughed and laughed.

Four months later, still recovering from my experience in the ICU and adapting to a life totally reliant on taking medication,

I was laid off from my job. To retain the same health insurance plan I paid $60 a month for through my company was $800 a month, paid for on my own. I had to cash out my 401(k) in order to pay for it, because unemployment was just $340 a week (rent alone was $550 a month). If I went just sixty days without some kind of insurance, my condition would be considered "preexisting" and I would become uninsurable for twelve to twenty-four months even through an employer-sponsored plan. So I had to find some way to pay for health insurance—health insurance that still didn't even pay 100 percent for my drugs. So it was $800 a month for my premium *plus* another $300 a month for the only partially covered drugs. This was just to stay alive. To keep my head above water.

I picked up temp jobs, and after getting through my thirty days with them, was able to sign up for some shitty insurance that technically covered me (so I wouldn't fall between plans and get hit with the preexisting thing), but didn't pay for my medication. So I was still paying out of pocket for that while trying to pay rent. Credit cards became my friend. I had four of them. Eventually, this situation became unsustainable, and in March of 2007 I packed up all my shit and moved to Dayton, Ohio, where I lived in a friend's spare bedroom, rent-free, while trying to live on expired insulin and checking my blood sugar the minimum amount possible to save on the cost of the testing strips, which were $1 apiece and which I was supposed to be using seven to eight times a day.

Without the temp agency I'd been at before in Chicago, I found myself uninsured once again while trying to rack up the requisite number of temp hours I needed from my new temp agency to qualify for their shitty insurance, which, once again, wouldn't cover my medication anyway. So it didn't make a difference to how much I was spending on drugs (most of my medication costs were going on a credit card at this point). But it did start the "preexisting condition" clock running again. I only had sixty days to get insured again, but I wasn't getting enough hours yet to qualify for the new temp agency plan.

I was sick, my medication was working sporadically since it was expired, and my credit cards were rapidly getting maxed out. I was mostly unemployed and only technically not homeless because I had a friend with a spare bedroom. I just stopped looking at my credit card statements. Being in debt, I figured, was better than being dead. But I knew that if I didn't get lucky at some point soon, I was going to end up dead regardless.

I signed up with another temp company, but was still sixty days out from being able to use their insurance. I ended up twisting my ankle and had to go to the ER. The bill was $800. When I got it, I just looked at it and laughed. I never paid that bill. I had to go back to the ER again with an issue related to my IUD. That bill was $600. I laughed at that one too, and didn't pay it.

I could pay those ER bills, or pay for the medication that kept me alive. Easy choice.

My temp company had me working an assignment for three months at a local company. I finally went to the temp company and said, "Listen. I can't pay for the medication that keeps me alive. Either these people need to hire me or I need to get a full-time position somewhere else." I went to my employer and said the same.

The temp company and my employer got together and—bless their hearts—my employer bought out my contract from the temp agency. My salary was just $32,000, and I didn't negotiate at all, because I got first-day health benefits. And the premiums were free. Yes, free—the company paid 100 percent of the premiums and there was no deductible. I immediately ordered new drugs—the drugs that kept me alive—and paid nothing for them.

That company saved my fucking life. My spouse sometimes

wonders why I still do freelance work for them, and why I don't charge them the rates I do everyone else.

It's because they saved my fucking life.

But because they saved my fucking life, they also got me for a really good deal. At that point, things were so bad I would have worked for nothing. I would have just worked for the health insurance. Their insurance plan was so good, in fact, it was a common joke over there: "Hey, if you lay me off, I'll work for free. Just let me keep my health insurance!"

But today, that shit is over. Today, you don't have to joke about working for a company for free, just to get the health insurance.

Today, you don't have to juggle eight credit cards to get the medication you need to live.

Today, for the first time in the United States, you can sign up for health insurance no matter how much money you make, no matter what your health condition—even if you have cancer, or you had cancer, or you've got some shitty immune disorder like mine. You don't have to go to bed on some shitty mattress in some friend's basement hoping and praying that you'll get some lucky break before your expired medication stops working. You don't have to beg a company to hire you just for the health benefits.

Today you don't have to pay $800 a month for bare minimum coverage, and cash out your 401(k) and live on expired medication. You don't have to run up multiple credit cards with medical bills. You don't have to cry when the bills from the ER come in.

You can go to healthcare.gov and find a health plan that works for you. Can't afford it? That's okay. The government will subsidize plans for people who can't pay for them. You don't have to worry about being unemployed and homeless and dying of some treatable thing in an alley somewhere.

You don't have to hope you'll get lucky—hope that some

friends will take you in and an employer will show you mercy. All you have to do is be a human being. And you'll be treated like a human being.

I don't wish my experience on anyone. It's my fervent hope that nobody in the United States ever has to live with the fear and terror I did during that year from 2006 to 2007 when my whole world imploded. I want people to forget what it's like to live that way. I want them to think that this is the kind of story you'd only hear about in some SF dystopia novel. And I don't want it to be a story that anybody in the country ever has to live again.

Becoming What You Hate

WHEN I WAS EIGHTEEN I WAS LIVING IN A SHITTY apartment, far from home, with an emotionally manipulative boyfriend. I felt totally powerless in my own life. I contemplated suicide often. I would learn, later, that taking birth control pills had caused a debilitating state of depression, one I simply could not shake no matter how much I willed it. Being mentally fucked up by my medication and entangled in an ongoing bullshit relationship with an asshole left me feeling I had no control over my own life.

So I decided to be someone else.

I did what a lot of teenagers did, when feeling out of control and powerless over their own lives in the late '90s:

I created an online persona.

Let's call him Adam, for simplicity's sake.

Adam was several years older than me. Confident. Tall. Wiry. Cocky. Single, of course. He was a funny flirt, a writer, and after conversing with some SF/F writers in an online forum for six months, he got invited to edit an early online magazine, which I did for the next six months.

Being Adam was a fabulous escape from my shitty life. It was the one place I could feel confident, because I was being some-body else. But giving myself that confidence boost meant dup-ing a lot of people. Flirting with a lot of women who thought I was a hot twenty-something dude (and probably a lot of forty-year-old dudes pretending to be women) and spinning tales about a life I certainly did not have. And I did that with many people who were being open and honest with me in return. It was the Wild West of the internet, though, and I didn't take much at face value. I had learned in the early days of the internet that you could be far more confident and get taken more seriously there than anywhere else at that age. I remember getting into conver-sations with people in online forums when I was fifteen, and hav-ing them speak to me as if I were an adult. It was addictive. It was an escape. It was fabulous.

It was all a lie.

Now, to be honest, Adam didn't say things like the anonymous internet persona known as Requires Hate, the sometimes-reviewer-sometimes-ranter who has been known to say that author so-and-so should have acid thrown in their face, or such-and-such should have his dick cut off, but I conversed with several writers in the field (and interviewed a couple of them!) as this dude, and edited stories as this dude. I went around telling lies to people, because it was too painful for me to be anyone else but a fictional character.

Eventually I escaped my shitty relationship, and quit editing the magazine, which went defunct soon after. I needed that per-sona to survive that year and change, though, and it worked. It reminded me there was a life outside myself, one I could build. If I had the strength to be that confident as Adam, I could learn to be that confident as Kameron.

I started my blog in 2004, after traveling around the world and getting a couple of fancy academic degrees. I'd gone out and built the life I wanted, and I was ready to be me. But I had to become someone I didn't hate before I could do all that.

I've spent over a decade learning to rein in my anger, my resentment, my hatred for people, for situations, for bullshit. I used to get into angry screaming fights in my teens. I'd lose my temper at the sound of loud voices. I'd snap, lash out, grind people under my boots. It wasn't until I was twenty-seven or twenty-eight that I realized I wanted a real healthy human relationship that lasted, and that if I wanted to do that, I had to learn patience, compromise, discipline.

I had to learn to talk out the seething anger. I had to learn where it came from, and stop trying to destroy people with it. I learned my limits. I figured out I was severely introverted, and that when I was ready to lose my shit, I needed to tap out instead, and retreat to a dark place to gather myself again. Much of my anger, I realized, was driven by anxiety and fear. When I'd remove myself from overwhelming social situations, I was better able to manage it.

But all this took time.

I had a lot of growing up to do.

I'm still angry a lot. I use tactical anger in many essays. But when I lose my shit now, it has a purpose. It's no longer just blind rage on the internet. Confidence helped with that, but mostly it was just getting older; it was getting a chronic illness; it was finding that the life I was living was not how I wanted to live, and changing it.

I was lucky in that I could do that. I had the resources at my disposal. My parents are solidly middle class. I have academic degrees. I've been working regularly since I was sixteen. I'm white, I'm reasonably presentable, my physical limitations are not obvious.

I made the choice to change my life, and with those resources, and my own will, I was able to do it. But it was a hard slog, learning not to lash out at everything with hate. Learning to be somebody I liked.

In my early days of reviewing on my blog, back when it was called *Brutal Women*, I said exactly what I thought of the bullshit sexism I saw in books. I received more than one angry email or comment from an author who thought my hurting their feelings by calling them out for writing a sexist book was some kind of crime, as if I'd actually physically taken a knife to them myself, when in fact it was their own ego-driven Google search that had led them to my review, and their own eyes that had continued to read it, and their own fingers that had typed up the email to send to me so they could engage with me and hear my opinion, once again, firsthand, delivered to their inbox at their request.

Emailing me to argue about whether or not your book is sexist after I already said so online? Dick move, my friend.

That said, time heals many rifts. Many perceived hurts. Many perceived wounds. Or they at least scar over. And I am, at least, on "colleague" terms with all those folks today.

Though I have scaled back those honest reviews, I miss them sometimes. I miss saying what I really think. I'd be lying if I told you I didn't occasionally consider creating another persona, a pseudonym, who could speak the raging, blinding, ballsy truth I want to piss all over the internet some days.

But I realize this is my career. I'm a grown-up. I suck it up. I save the pseudonym for another day.

I carry on.

Having lived on the other side of the review divide, I have a particularly healthy(?) relationship with angry reviews of my own work, in particular the sort of angry reviews that have reached the level of those by Requires Hate, who was known for writing seething, hate-filled, pus-spewing reviews full of such vitriol that they were both horrifying and entertaining in equal measure. I eventually had to block that reviewer because people kept RT-ing her on my Twitter timeline, and my life was just too short to wallow in the mean-spiritedness of it all. And yet when Requires Hate reviewed *God's War*, it was not a big deal at all to me. The review boiled down to "This book is so fucking white it's whitey white white written by a white person" and I'm like, well, yeah, that's true. You really can't debate or cry about that. And the buried, useful parts weren't anything I didn't already know. I shrugged and moved on, because let's be real, my friends, I've read worse reviews of my books, and I've written some pretty angry reviews of other people's books.

I'm an adult with book deadlines. I move on. I have shit to do.

The reviews by Requires Hate hurt the writers who read them, sure (don't ego-search!), and turned off a lot of readers who might have otherwise bought the book. But they also hurt the reviewer who reviewed them, in the same way I was hurt by all those sexist novels I ranted about back in 2004 to 2006. I understood the feeling, even if I was put off by how it was delivered. It may have lost folks some readers, just like a bad book review at any other blog, but it didn't ruin anyone's career. The hurt was not a real knife to the throat, but hurt feelings by pointing out perceived failures for the entertainment of a horde of readers looking for a public savaging of someone's work.

It turns out that I'm a big kid, and if I don't want to read reviews like that, I don't have to read them. So I didn't.

I blocked Requires Hate. I didn't read the blog.

I moved on.

At the end of 2012, I read an astonishingly beautiful short story that had me so enthralled that I read the whole thing on my phone, hiding it under my desk at work so I could finish. It was the sort of fiction I wished I was talented enough to write. I saw a lot of the same themes that fascinated me—war, relationships between women, SFnal worlds that felt more like fantasy. But it was from a gifted writer who knew how to turn a phrase with far more beauty and passion than I'd ever been able to.

It was mind-blowing, heart-wrenching to see writing that good. I fell in love with it immediately.

It turned out that the author's work was all like that—exceptional, intricate, lovely. I voted for her for the Campbell Award without hesitation, and told everyone else to as well. I followed her on Twitter. We had lovely conversations. She tweeted about bees and makeup and beautiful stories.

She was fabulous. The writing was sublime. I was in love.

It was all a lie.

Back in 1967, a writer named Alice Sheldon created a whole new life, an entire persona, called James Tiptree, Jr. She managed this fiction for many years. Robert Silverberg famously said of Tiptree, "It has been suggested that Tiptree is female, a theory that I find absurd, for there is to me something ineluctably masculine about Tiptree's writing."

Sheldon found a particularly beautiful world in that persona, for many reasons, among them the confidence and freedom it brought. After she was outed as Tiptree in 1976 (after fans saw a letter of Tiptree's about his mother dying in Chicago, they looked up the obituary and made the connection), she said, "My secret world had been invaded and the attractive figure of Tiptree—he *did* strike several people as attractive—was revealed as nothing but an old lady in Virginia."

Being outed was devastating, but the secret, like all secrets, was bound to come out, and Sheldon must have known that as much as Requires Hate did when she decided to turn her hand at publishing fiction in the very venues she'd critiqued, befriending the very authors whose work she'd been shiv-grindingly reviewing for the lulz. The house of cards always comes tumbling down.

Sometimes you are well prepared for it. Sometimes you've completed the transition and moved on, as I had with Adam. Sometimes you haven't.

When secrets come out, sometimes people feel betrayed. I'm sure Silverberg felt sort of silly, probably the way I felt at being duped when I learned the writer who wrote the fiction I loved was the same one pissing vitriol all over the internet. I was lucky in that I got to sit with the uncomfortable knowledge that it was very likely the same person for several months before it was confirmed. It gave me time to digest the anger, sure, but more than that—the grief. I physically grieved for an online character I'd developed an affection for the previous two years. It was like losing a real person.

The idea was actually brought to my attention by the writer herself in a DM conversation that someone was looking to draw a connection between the two of them, and when she admitted to knowing about the Requires Hate review of *God's War*, I felt a clench of sadness, because the sort of writer she pretended to be online was not the sort of person who would know about that review.

But Requires Hate would. Because Requires Hate had written it.

The manipulation was masterful. I often wonder if Requires Hate has a day job, because let me tell you, it all sounds super exhausting to me.

On the internet, no one knows who you really are. You can be anyone you want to be. Some of us are better at pulling that off than others.

In my heart of hearts, I'd hoped it would all go away. God knows people like Harlan Ellison have been saying the dumbest, most abusive and hateful shit for years and no one seems to fucking care, even when they assault another writer onstage. But for some reason folks were really, really upset that a woman who ranted angrily on the internet for the entertainment value of a few hundred people was going to be successful by pure virtue of how great her writing was.

Somehow duping everyone into thinking they were some nice person was a hateful crime against humanity, as if we all haven't been pretending to be somebody else on the internet ever since there was a fucking internet.

Doxxing—the revealing of someone's personal information on the internet—to me always screams of punishment. It screams of anger. Of fighting hate with hate. Burning someone down to make yourself feel better. It's someone screaming angrily that if they can't be happy, no one can be happy. It's screaming like a shrieking toddler, because somebody who said their cookies were shit is now making great cookies.

It's them sounding like a fucking bitter jerk.

Life is a game. Some people are masters at it. Life, succeeding at life, is about manipulation, about being the best, about connections and networking. Any rich white dude will tell you that with pride. Many of the writers we uphold as being absolute paragons of the field are screaming racist misogynists who've done far worse than write an angry review on the internet or tell people in an email what they really think of their book. They are people who've physically abused and assaulted women in the field for years, pinched asses, raped women, told women writers in person that they weren't worth the shit on their shoe, and we buy their work. We praise their work. We put it on reading lists and say, "Yes, Lovecraft is indeed a racist, but he's a product of his time!" and make awards in their likenesses.

We make excuses for men. We make room for men.

You should keep being Tiptree. You aren't the same if you're Sheldon. Sheldon is just an old woman from Virginia. We can burn Sheldon down and erase her.

In truth, many writers are assholes. They aren't people you want to go to tea with. I don't like people, generally. I find them exhausting. I don't want to be friends with Harlan Ellison or Larry Correia or Orson Scott Card. Nick Mamatas has been one of the genre's biggest fucking trolls for ten years, and nobody blacklisted him or sent around a petition, and when he's got his asshole meter turned down, he too can be terribly entertaining on the internet.

But they are dudes, and that's expected. It's their place to be assholes. To be shit-stirrers. We make excuses for them, and their behavior.

We are assholes for doing it. But we do it.

There is a lot of hate in the world. A lot of righteous anger. We spew a lot of words at people, saying stuff like, "Who the fuck do you think you are?" We get angry for feeling hurt, for feeling duped, when the best way to respond when someone plays a masterful game is, quite simply, this:

"Well played. You're a remarkable writer. I wish you the greatest success in your career."

We say that shit because we are fucking adults. Because the writing is good. We're not here to be friends. I don't like a lot of writers. But when their writing is not bullshit, I still read it, quite often. The persona may be a lie. All of them may be a lie. Shit, the work may even be a lie! But we are not in love with pixels on the internet; we are not in love with the ideas of people and their petty fucking feuds and scrambling attention-grabbing. We are in love with the work.

Boycott whatever you please. Get angry at me for duping you, you four writers I interviewed back when I was Adam, but if you are going to blacklist people for being duplicitous, or for giving their opinion on the internet, or emailing you their opinion when asked, then you better blacklist me too.

Our actions have consequences. I'm all for consequences, and I support you saying, "Fuck that, I'm never reading that asshole again, not letting them join my club, and cutting off all contact." Perfectly fair and healthy, desirable, even! But going beyond that, reaching for the pitchforks and torches to destroy somebody? Maybe consider why it is you're ready to burn someone alive. Is it because they put a knife to your throat, or because you're angry and hurt that they said something true? Are you angry because you were duped? Because they're talented? Because they played a good game? Do you just want to burn it all down in hate, in retaliation, like a fucking asshole in turn?

The abyss, my friends. Don't stare too long in it. You get to choose the person you want to be, so you better choose wisely.

Because let me tell you this, to achieve what you want—the blacklisting, banning, burning, the destruction of another human being's success, transforming yourself into everything you despise—requires very little.

It requires only that you hate.

✖

Postscript: See Notes for further context.

Let It Go: On Responding (or Not) to Online Criticism

PEOPLE LOVE TO POINT ME TO BAD REVIEWS OF MY WORK on the internet. I suspect this is the same compulsion that gets people to say such extraordinarily bizarre things as, "This smells gross. Smell this!"

We all love a good meltdown. Shared experiences—whether outrage or the huffing of some reeking odor—bring us together. The more I try to keep my distance from online rage, the more I find people reaching out at me to poke the bear. Whether it's tagging me on various social sites when they share a review of my work, or fans sending me the link directly, the good, the bad, and the very, very ugly responses to my work are sure to find me, no matter how big a hole I dig to stay out of it.

I have learned when to read and respond, and when not to click, and when to walk away when a mob comes at me. In truth, there's very little said about me on the internet that I'm not aware of, even if I choose not to click a link for the full rundown, or read the comments. If I've said something in error, I apologize and strive to do better. If the apology is not accepted, I must move on, because there are some mobs that will never be sated. Knowing when to apologize and when you're being deliberately misread is a real skill, and something you learn with practice.

The truth is that online meltdowns (as opposed to apologies and moving on) in response to criticism always end badly. PR professional Justine Sacco, herself summarily fired for posting a racist tweet, took over a year to rebuild her career.[1] Author John Green was skewered for responding to a post from someone on Tumblr who called him "creepy" because he writes books about and for teen girls. Sacco has explained in subsequent interviews that the tweet was meant to be ironic. Green has committed to spending less time on Tumblr.[2] More spectacularly, Anne Rice had it out with readers in the comments section of Amazon, and went so far as to sign a petition to stop people from "bullying" authors via reviews.[3]

I've had people say all sorts of things about me online, many of which amuse me:

1. I'm a professional lesbian boxer (I wish).
2. I hate women/men.
3. I write feminist science fiction because it's "trendy."
4. I'm not a real feminist/I'm a straw feminist.
5. I'm an abuser.
6. I defend abusers.
7. I gaslight people (deny their lived experience).
8. I attack other writers to advance my career (pro tip: if you do this, it's actually a really bad way to advance one's career).
9. I don't actually understand women's roles in resistance movements (all I did was get a master's degree in that).
10. I don't believe internet abuse is real abuse (what?).

And that's just the clean version of the greatest hits. I told myself early on that mad things like the above weren't worth engaging with. If I did, I'd get accused of punching down at fans who had a right to say these things about me. And, you know, I agree: people have a right to say what they want about me. That's something you need to get, as a creator. You're not going to "win" any of these arguments. You are always seen as the person with the most power. Because these examples are tame in comparison to the author who spent months tracking down a Goodreads reviewer and showed up at her house to confront her, and the author who went to a reviewer's workplace and hit the reviewer over the head with a wine bottle. Authors still behave far more badly than many of their fans, and they often have the means and social capital to do it—and get paid to write a story about it.

That doesn't mean I don't get angry sometimes. My best defense against this stuff, I've found, is other fans. If I write very clearly online and state my positions in such a way that they're difficult to misconstrue, even those who willfully misconstrue them are generally corrected by other people who've read the same work.

The best example of this was a post I wrote about a notorious internet troll who came out as also presenting themselves as a new writer in the science fiction and fantasy field under another name (included in this collection as "Becoming What You Hate").

On the whole, the post was taken well, but there were a couple of people who read it very quickly or who read a sum-up someone else did online putting me into a "defends abusers" camp, and didn't read the article at all. When the internet draws lines, you have to stand by what you said, and disengage.

I reread the post several times to ensure it said what I wanted it to say. Satisfied with that, I had to admit that there were just going to be some people who insist on misreading a piece.

Over the next few days I watched as folks who had read the piece in-depth argued with those who had not. I stayed out of it. And by staying out of it and letting my words speak for themselves, I received three apologies from people—both on-line and privately—who had posted initially knee-jerk misread-ings of the post.

You have to stay out of it. Here's why:

Studies have shown that when politicians or celebrities make statements denying something, people are more likely to be-lieve they actually did the thing they're denying. You can't actu-ally say, "I deny ever going to Bolivia in September." People will immediately think, "Why does she need to deny going to Bo-livia? What happened in Bolivia? Something must have hap-pened in Bolivia!" Instead, you have to make an entirely new statement, something like, "In September, my family and I had a great time in New York City. We met with my friends Prinisha and Paul and had a fabulous time dining at this really great Co-lombian place." You go from denying a story (which becomes the story) to actually creating and sharing a new story that does the job of refuting the first without repeating it and giving it more steam.

This is a PR and communications trick that I've found I need to bring to my work as a writer. It's why when you ask a politi-cian a question, they often don't answer it. They wax on back to one of their talking points instead. Nixon famously did this with a speech about his dog, Checkers, that served as an effective answer to a question about a mismanagement of his campaign funds. In the media coverage after the speech, Checkers became the story, not the issue of financial improprieties.

What I've found is that many people delight in skewering and misreading you because they don't see you as a real person. You have become The Man. By bringing you down a peg they feel that they can claim a victory over everything you represent. I've had haters from all sides—far left, far right, and everywhere in between. You also become a focus for folks who are unhappy, or who feel powerless. You become this symbol of all the reasons they feel powerless and unhappy. Feminists in particular get this a lot from men who are generally but certainly not exclusively young and white. Young white men in the eighteen- to twenty-four-year-old range are often coming to grips with the fact that life isn't as easy as they were promised. I've been there myself. When you realize that life isn't going to hand you the job you want or the woman you want to fuck, you look around for someone to blame, and feminism becomes an easy target. If only women were subservient objects who stayed at home, there would be more jobs open to young white men and more women with no other option but to have sex with them for sustenance.

I realize that white-man utopia sounds really pleasing to these guys, but it's basically everyone else's worst nightmare. It's not so great for them, either, but they won't get that for a long time, if ever.

Suffice to say, you won't convince them of this in an online comments section, either.

This is why there are so many times when politic statements won't work, either, and the best response is no response.

The game of online hate is rigged against you as a woman and as a creator. I'm not saying this is great. It's not. It's shit. But understanding how the game is played can help you survive it. When things go wrong, you need to be able to step back and take the high ground. When I wrote an article for *The Atlantic* that took on both Gamergate and Sad/Rabid Puppy followers, I had two good days of muting people on Twitter ahead of me. I even had some guy support my Patreon just so he could send me an angry message about how the tweet of his that *The Atlantic* editors had included in the piece was misconstruing his position. I had people threaten me with legal action for libel. They called me all sorts of boring names. I knew that the worst thing I could possibly do was engage any of them, because if you engage one, the others smell blood.

I muted and muted and muted.

And then they got bored.

And it was over.

Sometimes the mob is just nonsense. You have to know when it's best to stand by your words and when to ride out the wave.

Your haters are not here for a conversation. They are here to keep you from doing your work.

In teaching a recent copywriting class, I spent an entire class lecture on how online harassment works, and why it's become a professional hurdle that every woman creator in particular must learn to navigate. For the record: I don't like that this is the case. But it's real, and we need to learn how to manage it.

When trolls are confronted about why it is they prey on people online, the most common response is "For the laughs." Anita Sarkeesian, the creator of the *Tropes vs. Women in Video Games* YouTube series, analyzed her own rabid trolls and found that many of them played trolling the way they would play a game. Folks got together and played for "points." Did you get a reply? How many people got angry with you? Did you make them angry enough to block you? Did they run away from their house? Did you get them to cry?

These are all points.

Trolling is a game.

Getting you to leave the internet, cry, talk about how hurt you are, leave your house, or (end goal!) kill yourself is the actual, for-real goal of many online trolls.

Because to them, it's just a game. It's a way to pass the time.

My approach to combating online trolling is to understand who it is who trolls. Studies have found that many trolls are pure sadists. They literally get pleasure from upsetting you. When

I see someone online who appears to be earnestly arguing a point with me who then says elsewhere that they are delighted with how they've gotten me to respond, to "froth" or "get angry" or "annoyed," I know I have a troll instead of a real conversation, and I disengage. Sadism is about feeling that one has power over someone, especially someone one or others admire, and power is a hell of a drug.

This is why I practically tear my hair out when I see the targets of trolling make big posts about how much trolling hurts them, and how depressed they get, and how it makes them not want to write, and how they cried themselves to sleep, or decided to use the internet less. The truth is that you are not actually doing what you hoped: you aren't proving your humanity to another human. You are simply telling the sadists that what they're doing is working. You're playing the game, now.

A lot of folks get angry when I point this out, that talking about how much trolling hurts is actually playing the troll game. Many argue that we must share the abuse we're getting online so that folks know it's real, and know what a heavy burden that women in particular bear by speaking publicly. I'm all about truth-telling and truth-sharing. If you need to put up a hate roundup a couple times a year or run a "death threats received" tally, okay. I get it. But if you're going to do that you need to understand that a lot of these people *live* for the hate roundup where you give their comment space on your blog or in a tweet. That's a point, folks.

That's the game.

Don't get me wrong—I'd love to see real consequences for hate speech that's meant to inspire terror and incite violence. And if we go after hate speech online, we would need to go after hate speech on the radio and on television, too, from big public figures who love to rile up their listeners in the hopes that they'll burn down the White House or a predominantly black church or become border-running vigilantes who shoot immigrants.

We would need to address why it is those who seek to incite hatred hide behind the flag of "free speech" and why it is you can hide there when you're talking about shooting up a black church or killing a woman online, but not blowing up an airplane or shooting up your school.

In the meantime we live in a world where someone threatening to rape or murder a woman for speaking publicly is treated with a shrug and a "boys will be boys" comment from law enforcement. And we need to learn how to survive in that kind of world.

I decided early on that I simply wasn't going to play the game.

Oh, certainly, I will occasionally paraphrase a ridiculous email, or I'll mention I had a few death threats during my early days online, but to be honest, after spending an entire decade building an audience for my work, I'm not going to give over that platform to some guy wanking off in his basement at the idea of getting girls to cry. I'm not giving them pages here or pixels there to reprint their bullshit.

They're going to have to do something of actual worth with their own lives to make headlines.

Alas, many still do by acting on those impulses. This is also why we need to begin to look at how we cover shootings, and acts of terror and violence against women. Yes, these things happen and we don't want to erase them, but the way the media covers acts of violence in this country often valorizes the person committing the crime. Instead of learning about the life of the victim and mourning their death, we get in-depth interviews with people about the killer. "Did you ever suspect . . ." "Oh no, no, he was always such a quiet boy!" etc. Our obsession with killers has bled over into our fictional media, too, with endless television shows that either have serial killers as protagonists (*Hanni-*

bal, Bates Motel, Dexter) or spend the entire episode trying to figure out their methods and psychoses, often positioning them not as quiet, powerless people but as attractive, suave, and intelligent men.

I was once on a panel at a convention where a writer said that she had stopped writing antiheroes because she found that most audiences could no longer tell the difference between a hero and an antihero, and I admit I'm leaning toward that sad conclusion as well.

We are giving over our time and attention and our hard-won platforms to people too frightened and angry to build lives for themselves that don't involve tearing down others.

And we need to stop.

There are many ways to silence a woman, and not all of them involve getting her to stop speaking. Sometimes it's enough to simply ensure all she speaks about is you.

When the Rebel Becomes Queen: Changing Broken Systems from the Inside

IN 2007, I WROTE AN ESSAY CALLED "WHY WRITING Colorblind Is Like Writing White" in response to a post by science fiction author John Scalzi. Scalzi wrote that his approach to writing about race in his work was to write "colorblind." He chose to use cultural and social cues to code the race of his characters without explicitly coding them as one race or another using identifiers like skin color, features, or hair styles. Back in 2007, I wasn't much of anybody worth listening to. I'd been to the Clarion West Writers' Workshop and published a few short stories, but I was known inside online feminist circles more broadly than I was known inside science fiction ones. Still, his point annoyed me, as I knew the default perspective that I and many other readers had been programmed to assume. So in my post I pointed out that the default reading experience for many of us in the United States is white and male, and trying to write "colorblind" was going to result in readers whitewashing the book. Other writers, including K. Tempest Bradford and Rachel Swirsky, pointed out the fallacy of this as well. Discussions were had. Points were made, and all of us, including Scalzi, ended up changing the way we wrote as a result of the discussion online.

I was Nobody, yelling online about a Somebody, and I was heard.

When those with perceived power listen, it can be shocking. You get used to yelling at walls. When they do turn around and change their behavior, you can stop yelling. Sometimes when you make a cogent argument, you get a real result. It's important to have voices out there willing to point out the errors or blind spots that creators have. It's important for creators to listen.

But once you stop yelling from outside the wall and climb over the other side, can you still effect real change, or are you destined to be subsumed into a system that often rewards lazy writing and bad behavior?

Over the last couple of years, I have gone from Nobody to Somebody, and after over a decade of being on the side of the nameless internet mob I've found that readers have put me on the other side of the fence. I'm not the one howling for justice anymore. I'm the one who's fucking up and needs to be called out. I'm the problem. I'm The Man.

It's really weird, to wake up one day and realize you're The Man, because you really don't feel like him and you're really not sure what to do with all this audience-granted privilege. In truth, very little about my life seems to have changed in all this time. I don't feel any more powerful. I make more money, but I dump most of that into debt I accrued while poor and into traveling to speaking engagements to try to sell more books to ensure I can get more book contracts. My life feels like one endless hustle. One big hamster wheel of write, edit, market, repeat.

It wasn't until I looked up from the wheel that I realized my perceived place in the hierarchy of things had changed, and I needed to alter my perception of myself to acknowledge how others perceived me. I have five novels out as I'm writing this, and two more coming out in the next year and a half. I've become someone whose voice reaches outside of my small real-world social circle to a far larger one made up of readers, fans, and industry professionals. If you have over one thousand Twitter followers you're in the top 5 percent of users. And if you sell more than five thousand copies of any one book, you're in the top 10 percent of published authors. I have both of those things, so I can't be as powerless and unexceptional as I generally feel.

Acknowledging that shift has been . . . difficult. I feel the same. I look the same. Well, maybe I look more tired.

The question becomes what it is one can do to change and improve these systems of power and privilege from the inside once one has "arrived." I certainly have a number of folks online crowding through my mentions and emails trying to tell me what it is I can and should do. The difficult part is sifting through those voices and figuring out when you've done something harmful and when the mob is just howling for blood and you're an easy target. Who's the next Kameron Hurley yelling at John Scalzi?

When my essay "We Have Always Fought" went viral, I had someone email me and note that there was a problematic line in the essay that erased trans women. When I reread the line, I found that they were right. I had. So I rewrote the line and included a nod to nonbinary folks as well. I could not very well write an essay about erasure and then proceed to erase an entire group of women who get erased far too often. It was a harmful thing I had done, contributing to a broken narrative, so I fixed it.

I am not perfect all the time. There are things I often don't see. I write very quickly, to deadline, like everyone else. But when I misspeak, or I see that something I've said has done harm, I am quick to apologize and correct it. That's not always enough for people who've been hurt. I get that. I have been one of those people. If a book goes out with a rape scene in it that's superfluous, or contributes to rape culture in some way, I'll be disappointed in that author and their work. That can't be avoided. If I'm dismissed by someone in conversation, or talked down to, or mansplained, it will rankle. There are authors on my shit list who won't come off it no matter how much they try to change. I recognize that I'm on someone's shit list too, and nothing I can do will change the hurt I caused them. I have to live with that. So do they.

I wanted to think I could maintain my outsider status even while benefiting from the very privilege that being a writer bestows. That just isn't going to happen. No matter how much of an outsider you feel, no matter how much you think you're the marginalized voice sticking it to The Man, the reality is that you're the Great Villain in somebody's story, and the minor villain in a bunch more. For every good you do, you do harm somewhere else.

Maybe sanity is simply accepting this truth, and carrying on regardless, and doing the best you can.

I spend a lot of time gnawing on this question: Is it really possible to change the world from inside of a corrupt system, or do you risk being devoured by it? I've been a cog inside the corporate machine since I was sixteen and got an admin job at the corporate office of the burger joint where my parents had worked their entire lives. I got introduced to corporate politics when both of my parents were laid off within twenty-four hours of each other. I quit the next day in solidarity, thinking my parents would be proud of me. Instead, they grilled me on what I had said when I gave my notice. Had I violated their confidentiality agreement? Were they going to lose their stock payouts?

My parents started their careers in the same place: a little family-owned hamburger chain with stores in Washington and Oregon. They worked their way up from line cooks to assistant

managers to managers to area managers to fancy corporate titles for a couple of years before the end. Those were good gravy
years, contrasting sharply with my early childhood memories of
living on scrambled eggs and macaroni and cheese.

But when I talk about how they worked their way up from line
cook to VP, I have to acknowledge that they were able to do that
because they were white. My dad was the first manager to ever
hire a black person at the restaurant chain, in 1977, and in order
to do that he had to get permission from the president of the
company. My parents were given opportunities others were not,
just as I've been given opportunities others have not. Yes, it's hard
work that got me here, but I benefited from a system that gave
me a leg up over some others.

It begs the question: Now that I'm on the inside, whether
or not I feel that way, am I doing anything to make the way here
easier for those coming up behind me? Am I signal-boosting
voices? Am I recommending books that might have been missed?
Or am I perpetuating the same old problems, and the same old
narratives, by supporting writers who the system has already
privileged on the way here? And, oh God, can I just say how much
I hate the word "privilege"? Because I do, and still I use it, because
it's such an easy stand-in for so many things.

What I've realized on my way here is that it's not only certain
types of people—middle and upper middle class, white, male—
who have the easier time, generally, just getting here. It's also
people with a certain type of personality, and I don't think this
gets talked about enough, either, while we're talking about various kinds of -isms and capital "P" privileges. Becoming a writer,
being able to sit here and pen essays for money, requires one to
have the ability to endure an astonishing amount of rejection.
One must either be very confident or have a personality that when
told "You're not good enough" responds by saying "Just you wait."

It takes a very confident and/or relentless person to get twenty years of rejection slips and not give up. You have to be legitimately odd to get tireless hatred spewed your way on the internet and in reviews, for years, and keep going.

I can tell you that you need to endure, but how many can or are willing to endure this bullshit just to make a living? And, a better question: Why the fuck should we have to? Why does this have to be part of the job description to type words on a page?

I got into writing because it was a solitary, introverted thing I could do on my own. There were few things I loved more than sitting at a keyboard all by my lonesome, hallucinating fabulous stories that I could put down in words and share with others. But share virtually, of course, because oh Lord I did not want to actually get up and speak to people and see their reactions to my stories. I wanted to share them quietly, from a great distance.

Being on the inside now means doing things I don't always like, because what no one tells you about getting into the writing game is that staying here is much, much more difficult than getting that first book published. If you haven't had a book published yet, you are snorting at me indignantly, but if you've had your first book published, you're nodding along sagely. I would argue that if you're a writer with a book that had poor sales, there's more standing in the way of you publishing a book than if you're a debut writer. And if that doesn't blow your mind, I don't know what else to tell you. The possibility for success of an unknown writer will always outweigh the known failure of a writer whose work performed poorly.

Joanna Russ, one of the most subversive science fiction writers I'd ever read, dropped out of the writing game in the early '90s after decades of writing and publishing feminist science fiction essays and novels. Many said she left the game for health reasons, and no doubt this was a large part of it. But as I get older, I understand why so many writers, especially women writers, throw in the towel and tell the industry to fuck itself.

We climbed our way up here over the wall, and now we're on the inside, and we find there are more hurdles, and higher walls, and we must not only throw ropes over the other side to help others after us, but also scale these new walls. What I never understood from the outside is how difficult it is to stay on the inside.

It's why I understand when I see my colleagues lash out in fear when they, too, are called out for problematic stories or tweets taken out of context, or legitimately dumb things they said while on deadline, while ill, while not taking the time to consider who it may hurt. I understand it, but I have also seen how to handle it—how we can turn critique into dialogue, and criticism into discussion. I believe in the potential of the mob, even if I disagree with many of its tactics.

Because as I have seen, having been on both sides of the wall, real change takes both sides coming together to have an honest conversation. An author can't pretend they're in an ivory tower, untouchable, perfect; and a yowling Nobody like me needs to know what the endgame is, and when an apology and a promise to do better is exactly what you hoped for.

For all my cynicism, I believe in the goodness of people. I believe we can get to a better world without destroying each other. I believe we can reach back, and throw the rope over, and pull others through to help us continue our climb, instead of trying to face the hurdles of a broken system alone as those before us did.

The reality is that you cannot change a system from the inside unless you, too, are willing to change. You must acknowledge that you're here to make it easier for those who come behind you, and you are going to knock down walls along the way that they won't have to scale. And you will need to love them still, and welcome them, even though they will not understand how much you fought, even though your paths to this place will be different. You must be all right with them hating you for being there ahead of them. You must be all right with becoming the one they associate with the system. You must be all right with becoming The Man. Because if you're the Great Villain, if you are all the evil that is in the world, then maybe, just maybe, it's a better place than it was when you tore down all the dinosaurs blocking the way ahead of you.

You can't avoid becoming the enemy. But you can be less of an enemy, a more welcoming villain, a force for good and change who fades quietly ahead of the onslaught of new, more powerful voices you helped over the wall. You can learn how to get out of the way, instead of impeding them.

Terrorist or Revolutionary?
Deciding Who Gets to Write History

BEFORE HE WAS THE FIRST DEMOCRATICALLY ELECTED president of South Africa and a symbol for peaceful resistance, Nelson Mandela was a terrorist.

This is not rhetoric, or a purposefully inflammatory statement. It's just fact. The government of South Africa and the U.S. government, among others, categorized the African National Congress, the party to which Mandela belonged, as a terrorist organization, and Mandela and his colleagues were terrorists. I spent nearly two years in South Africa studying South African resistance movements. I have seen the news clippings. I have been hip-deep in the narrative.

I think about this a lot when I watch the news. I think a lot about who gets to write history, and how who's the good guy and who's the bad guy can change depending on the day and the new enemy. Saddam Hussein was our dear friend in Iraq fighting the big bad Iranians who captured our embassy. He was our dear friend until he wasn't, and then we went to war with him. Osama bin Laden was initially trained by the CIA to fight the Soviet army. He was welcomed home by his family as a hero, and considered an asset to the United States.[1] And if one wants to imagine how our narrative of the Civil War would have been should the South have won, spend some time talking about the "War between the States" in the deep South.

How quickly our narratives change, depending on when and who is telling the stories.

This is not to excuse any of the things done by the tyrants of history, but it's important to remember that from my seat here in the United States, much of what we have done and are doing is tyrannical. The United States just bombed a Doctors Without Borders hospital in Afghanistan and murdered nineteen people.[2] Isn't that a terrorist act? Mandela blew up buildings too. American colonists employed guerilla tactics in the fight against the British. We were uppity, entitled people who didn't like taxes, so we went to war over it. It's a good thing we won, too, or that story would be far different. Bad things were done in the war for independence. Bad things were done during the colonization of this country. We committed genocide against an entire people. We rounded up people into concentration camps. We were an evil slave empire. The White House, symbol of supposed democracy and freedom, was built by slaves.

But we're the good guys, right?

The truth is that who and what is good and bad is highly dependent on who wins, and whose point of view we're writing from. This matters to me because I see how desperately we want to put ourselves and our history and heritage into neat boxes labeled good and bad. This is especially toxic for those, like me, who have grown up in a country that privileges white skin over all others, and has aggressively ensured that the paler one's skin, the more privileges one has. Systems of racism and sexism and oppression are not systems we choose, but they are ones we inherit and are responsible for perpetuating, or not. When I hear so-and-so was "a product of his/her time" as an excuse for bigoted behavior I remind folks that there have always been people in every time who did not agree with the bigoted systems they were born into and who actively fought them.

The question is, which are we? And are we willing to stand up against those systems, or say that they are just too big for us to confront? No doubt apartheid looked like an impossible system to overturn without a bloody revolution. And the British were still the most fearsome colonizers in the world when the American colonies broke away from them.

These systems are built on stories about their inevitability, about their power, about their enduring legacy. We tell stories about our own oppression that make oppression seem like a biological inevitability. An entire rhetoric was created around race to justify the slavery of black people in the Americas, just as we see an entire rhetoric dedicated to why women are not suited for anything but babies and making house. We are born and raised hearing these stories, and we internalize them as if they are truth.

But internalizing a story does not make it true.

When I challenge people to interrogate evil, and our narrative of terror and fear, I am in turn challenging them to interrogate their own self-narrative . . . and the narrative of the societies they grew up in. Because it is only by challenging these narratives that we will effect any change in the world.

So who are we if all the stories are made up? Who are we if what's monstrous or heroic is really just a matter of who's telling the story? Who owns our story?

We must own our own stories. We must tell our own truths. Without this, we will become casualties of our own governments' rhetoric, the court of public opinion, and inevitably, the history that others perpetuate.

This is why I write. This is why I keep speaking. This is why I endure. Because if I don't tell my stories, someone else will.

Giving Up the Sky

I WENT HIKING AT THE PARK RECENTLY, AND FINISHED up the five-mile jaunt in an open meadow, sitting in an Adirondack chair that forced me to gaze up at the sky. For a long moment I was transfixed by the billowy puffs of clouds moving slowly across the flat blue sky. When was the last time I'd stopped to look, really look, at the sky? I'm in my midthirties now, hurtling quickly toward middle age in a life I felt I only really started living in my twenties.

I remember being ready to leave the house at thirteen, frustrated by my lack of legal autonomy and my loving but worried parents whose permission generally didn't extend beyond letting us play at the neighbor's house for a few hours. My great-grandfather had left his own home at thirteen and traveled across the country by hitching a train, and made his living shining shoes and doing odd jobs. Clearly my life was very different.

At seventeen, I tried to leave the house amicably, figuring I was close enough to legal age to jump, but my parents (rightly) insisted that I needed to be eighteen before I could leave. By the time I got out of there I was practically crawling out of my skin to get away. Not because I had a terrible house life or my parents hated me; quite the opposite. I was aware that my childhood had been a carefully constructed bubble of minimal strife and unhappiness, and I knew that my insulation from the real world meant that I had no idea what I was really made of. I didn't know what I could really do, or if I could deal with real problems. Could you say you were strong if you never had to be?

My first year out of the house, predictably, was a spectacular failure. Laid low by serious depression induced by birth control pills and desperately trying to make my way at a hostess job while I went to community college classes, my relationship with my mad, misguided high school boyfriend eventually imploded too. His grandmother stopped supporting him, and he ran off to join the Marines, leaving me with an apartment I couldn't afford on my own and a car I didn't have insurance on. When I got a $500 ticket for driving without insurance and had my phone turned off because I couldn't pay the bills, I knew eviction was next. The notice on the door didn't surprise me. I walked a mile to the nearest pay phone and used change I'd scrounged from the seats of the car to call my parents and asked them to drive the five and a half hours to come get me. I pawned everything I could, and my dad and brother came and picked up the rest. We didn't say a word about my failure at being an adult. There wasn't even an "I told you so."

I had realized exactly where my blind spots were. I'd never been taught to budget or deal with relationship conflict. I had no idea how to manage my finances or connect with potential roommates. I'd never even signed up to rent movies before. I had no knowledge of how utilities were set up and paid for. Here I was with all this education and supposed "smarts" that people had been praising me for since I was a kid, but I had no idea how to take care of myself in the real world. I had no idea how the real world worked.

I wonder sometimes what would have happened if my parents hadn't taken me back. Would I have ended up on the street, or found a room to let and persevered? Was I even mentally equipped to do that? Probably not while that depressed, no. The lesson I learned the second time around, when I left the house at nineteen to go to college at the University of Alaska Fairbanks, was that I needed to figure out these very basic ways of taking care of myself. And I needed to figure out how to do that without relying on anyone else to manage it for me. I'd trusted in my boyfriend to handle the apartment and the utilities and the car, and when he failed at that, I had no idea what to do about it. If I was going to make it, I didn't need to learn about partnership; I needed to learn, first, to take care of myself without anyone's help.

It's no surprise that this was also the same time I discovered feminism. How had I fallen into this weird trap? Why did I rely on my parents and my boyfriend to handle everything? Why was I constantly trying to be this good girl who listened to what everyone else thought was good for her?

Nobody else was going to provide me with transportation, or half the rent. No one else was going to save me out there in Alaska but myself. I resolved that I would never have to call my parents to come and get me ever again.

There is a self-loathing that comes with knowing you are soft, breakable, unprepared. And there are two ways you can deal with that. You can cry into your cornflakes and accept it, or you can remake yourself.

When I moved to Alaska I said yes to every opportunity. I accepted a ride from a stranger. I learned to bowl and to roll my own cigarettes. I learned to hot-wire cars. I drank too much and went on stupid dates. I learned to shoot while drunk. I made out with some questionable characters. I used an outhouse at forty below. I spent five days in a cabin on the coast with a guy I'd only been out with once, and went hiking into the middle of nowhere with him and his friends. I drove out to part of the Arctic Circle in the middle of the night and spent hours in a car stuck in a snowdrift, drinking beer and smoking to keep from freezing.

My parents were not impressed when they saw pictures of the people I was consorting with, but I needed something different. I needed to acquire skills and tackle challenges that good, nice, middle-class kids didn't deal with. Living in Alaska was the happiest time in my life, and I remembered, as I stared up into the sky fifteen years later, it was also the last time I had looked up at the sky like this. I'd sit out in the big field adjacent to the university and just lie out there and look at the sky while the wind rushed through the birch trees. I grew so attached to the sound of those white birches that I planted three of them at my house in Ohio.

In many ways, I feel that I have gotten soft again. I traveled throughout my twenties—eight different countries—and moved nine times in nine years. When people ask me what stopped the constant moving, I admit it had a lot to do with getting tired of moving all of my books. I started to fantasize about permanent bookshelves. Simple as that.

The more interesting question is why it took fifteen years for me to stop and see the sky again. Have I been afraid to look up, afraid to stop, to see what I've become? By all accounts I have a large measure of the success I strove for when I was seized by the need to leave my house at thirteen. On the other hand, the cost of this success, particularly during the last four or five years, has been ceaseless work and hustle on a scale I never imagined. There has been less travel, and the word "yes" only leaves my mouth in response to writing gigs and speaking engagements, not camping trips and tree climbing.

I've gone from wandering free spirit to calculating business-person, and though I very much enjoy not being evicted or scrounging for money in my car, I wonder sometimes if it's worth giving up the sky.

REVOLUTION

What We Didn't See:
Power, Protest, Story

MY PARENTS TAUGHT ME NOT TO STARE.

As children, even as adults, prolonged staring at others is something we do when we first encounter difference. It's a long, often critical or fascinated look at something to try to understand it, to gauge where it fits in our taxonomy of things. First: Is this a threat? Should I respond with a fight . . . or flight? Second: Where does this person fit within my existing boxes? Woman or man? Black or white? Friend or foe?

We have nice, neat boxes for everything—boxes we learned in childhood that have been reinforced as we grew older by stories, by media, by our peers. We stare longest when we cannot fit what we see into an existing box, when we cannot figure out if it's dangerous, or merely different—which many of us, unfortunately, still feel are the same thing.

And if, after staring long enough, we decide that this different thing is dangerous, we kill it.

I grew up in a town that was about 98 percent white.[1] I would learn, decades later, that it was purposely constructed that way, as were many other places in the United States. (California went so far as to ban the immigration of free and enslaved blacks into the state,[2] though that did not prevent those already there from continuing to eke out a living. Also see: the exclusion laws of Oregon.[3, 4])

When I was three or four years old, my family took me to Reno, Nevada. We stayed at the Circus Circus Hotel, and while my dad went downstairs to play cards, my mom ordered up a special treat: cheesecake, delivered in a way totally new to me—via room service.

The knock came on our door. My mom opened it. And there was a very dark man in a very white coat holding a silver-colored tray.

"Mom!" I said, three or four years old and having never seen anyone much browner than a pale person with a suntan. "Why is that man so *black*?"

My mom, mortified, laughed and hushed me and tipped generously, I learned later. These were not polite questions. They revealed where and how I'd grown up. The question revealed the constructed lie of how we lived.

When he was gone, she told me, simply, that some people were born with different colors of skin, like different colors of hair. Being three or four years old, I was perfectly contented with this answer, and went on to happily eat my cheesecake. It would be four or five years more before I realized that in our society, skin color was not seen in the same way hair color was, even if, in my kid's view of the world, it made exactly the same amount of difference as blue eyes or brown, red hair or black.

Even a child cannot escape history. We can't escape what came before us.

Looking back, the irony is not lost on me, of course: the irony that the first person of color I ever saw, as a white child, was a black man serving me cheesecake on a polished platter.

* * *

Difference has been managed in a variety of ways, across times and cultures. Because difference is, of course, in the eye of the beholder. The *Twilight Zone* episode "Eye of the Beholder" posits a world where beauty itself is interrogated as a construct.[5] A female patient spends nearly the entire episode covered in bandages while her doctors converse with her, always with their own faces out of sight, in shadow. In the end, it's revealed that the woman has a movie-star beauty of a face: pale skin, pale hair, sparkling eyes, pleasingly symmetric features.

Hollywood beauty. The beauty our American culture, collectively, is told to strive for—even if it is so far beyond and outside what any of us actually look like.

Her doctors, nurses, the "normal" people in her world, are revealed to have the melted-looking faces of deformed pigs. They are the beautiful ones. She is the anomaly.

She is the difference.

In the end, she is shuttled off to a concentration camp. A ghetto created for people of her "kind." They say she will be happier there, among those like her. Most importantly, though, she will be hidden from the eyes of those unlike her. They will be free from seeing her ugliness.

Her difference makes them uncomfortable, and for that grave crime, she must be locked away.

Sometimes difference from a culturally defined norm is celebrated—a mark of the gods, divine. Sometimes it is feared—a mark of evil. But most often, in the culture we call American, what we've done the last couple hundred years is lock up[6] and shutter away[7] and refuse to showcase all but the very narrow subset of humanity those in power would like us to believe are the true normal. This dangerous lie has led to the dehumanization of millions, and people who are dehumanized are not simply written out of the cultural narrative. They are, very often, utterly and literally[8] removed from the face of the earth.

I have written before about how our broken sense of what is "normal" feeds into dangerous narratives, and how it limits the lives of women.[9]

But the reality is, this system of stories goes far beyond rewriting history to limit how we believe women fought, or lived. These stories—that there is this very narrow subset of "normal" people: upper middle class, white, women being women, men being men—serves to make the rest . . . not. Anyone who doesn't fit is, of necessity, abnormal.

"Abnormal" often meaning "not human."

And not human . . . well, we know what we do to things that aren't human, don't we?

The fastest way to dehumanize a person, or a subset of people, is to make them invisible. To lock them away. To say, "This is the stuff of circuses and mistakes. This is the stuff of nightmares."

It's easier to reject,[10] fear,[11] and destroy[12] what we don't understand.

It's impossible to understand what we're never allowed to see.

Even if, in many cases, what we never see is *ourselves*.[13]

I passed a man and his son headed to a football game one day. The news was, at the time, all about the protest and unrest in the city of Ferguson, Missouri, where peaceful protests in reaction to the shooting of an unarmed teenager were met with an increasingly violent police response.

One would think there would be a profound backlash against this militarized police response, no matter the race of the victim.

But one would be wrong.[14]

The boy and his father crossing the street to the stadium were white; the boy was about eight or nine years old, and he asked, "Dad, what if it had been a black cop shooting a black kid? What about a white cop shooting a white kid? Why are people upset because it was a white cop shooting a black kid? Would it be different another way?"

There was an uncomfortable moment of silence from the father, and when he responded, I could hear the tension in his voice. "I don't know," he said.

I don't know.

These two people, likely growing up in neighborhoods as artificially constructed as the one I lived in, had no reason to know. They had not spent their lives terrorized by police the way that nonwhite people are.[15] They had not had loved ones shot in the street outside of their homes, as continues to happen in largely black and immigrant communities. They had not grown up in neighborhoods where simply looking the way they did meant they were quite likely to spend a great deal of their time in prison.[16] The statistics, for these two people—a white boy, a white man—were very different than for others.

Of course they don't know.

People in power don't want them to know. They want these people's allegiance against the Other.

Divide and conquer is a time-tested strategy. Divide and conquer works.[17]

How do you explain four hundred years of prejudice, oppression, exclusion laws, and terror to an eight-year-old middle-class white boy on the way to a football game?

The truth is, he will likely never see it. Never even notice it.

And that's the fault of mainstream stories. It's the fault of our laws. It's the fault of the culture we call "ours" but that isn't really representative at all. It is the culture of a select few, assumed to be the culture of many.

But "us" is the fiction. "Ours" is the lie.

Who is "us"?

My academic advisor in graduate school was born with phocomelia, a rare congenital disorder that results in atypical formation of the limbs. We went into town one day to print and bind copies of my hundred-and-some-odd-page thesis, and she popped into a fabric shop to run an errand before we went to the printer.

I remember seeing a young child at the counter, standing next to his mother, staring at my advisor, whose shorter arms and legs made her much smaller than him. His eyes were so big. Staring. Forever and ever. No break. Goggle-eyed.

I remember being irrationally angry at this child for staring, and I stepped between him and my advisor to shield his view.

Now, I couldn't tell you why I did it. She had to deal with these stares every day, and worse. It was me who was angry. It was me who was uncomfortable. It was me frustrated with how we notice and process difference.

My mother always told me not to stare. It was rude. It said, "You are different." And difference, acknowledging difference, was bad. To acknowledge difference was to acknowledge everything that was broken. Yet . . . how was pretending not to see someone any better?

In truth, what was being protected by not seeing was my naïve four-year-old question that revealed how I was raised: "Why is that man so *black*?" Staring said we were rural simpletons with a limited view of the world. It wasn't the difference itself that was terrible to acknowledge, for my parents, I think; it was acknowledging the fact of our own ignorance.

But the gaze, the stare, as many women know, can also be seen as a prelude to an assault. We fear and sometimes covet what we see. And what we fear and covet, often, we will violently assault.

I feared that stare. Even from a child who knew nothing of its historical implications.

I saw myself in his stare.

And that made me angry.

So what is it that we don't see? That we have stopped seeing? That we don't want to see?

What we don't see has a great deal to do with who we are, how we grew up. It has to do with how our society manages the ebb and flow of people; what it considers different, undesirable.

Whether we believe we're living in a dystopia today depends on where we're sitting.

A banker's utopia is a factory worker's dystopia. Utopic gated communities that do not permit low-income residents are utopic only for the few who live there. They do not fix the wider problem of crime and poverty. They simply push it out to the fringes, where they can't see it.

But unseeing a thing doesn't make it disappear.

In truth, pushing people aside, locking them away, putting them into ghettos, erasing them from stories does far more harm than any amount of seeing will do.

Because what we see we actually have to acknowledge as a part of the wider story, the wider culture.

What we see is *us*.

I write stories. It's what I do. It's what my colleagues do. By day I craft marketing and advertising copy that's still mostly white, mostly ableist, mostly upper middle class, assumed heterosexual. Mostly male.

But as the voices we see and hear every day become harder to ignore, harder to unsee, that is changing too. I can put different people onto the page, and use different language—not just at my day job, but at my night job, too. My novels can give you a hero of either or other or no gender, from a variety of cultures of every type and hue and practice. My heroes can have limitations of mind, of body, limitations imposed at birth, by circumstance, or by society and still be heroes. They can be all of this and more.

They can be *seen*.

And publishers will buy them. And readers will read them.

My fear of being unpublished, pushed out, ignored because of who or what I write about is fading.

This is changing not because the people themselves are there any more or less than they (we!) used to be. The world has always been a diverse and interesting place. But with the rise of social media and instant communication platforms, it's easier to organize and speak out. It's easier to come together. It's easier to insist on being *seen*. It's harder to forget or wipe away the history that brought us all to the places we started this life within, the cultural constructs that bound us. The constructs we are working so hard to unmake, refute, challenge.

So if you find yourself wondering why so many of us ask to be included now, and put ourselves and others into stories we've been written out of, perhaps first ask why that inclusion is considered political, but the erasure was not: the laws, the asylums, the housing policies, the repression, the abuse.

There is nothing more political than erasure. Than *unseeing*.

The world is not changing. It's been this way all along. We have been here all along. All that's changing is what you *see*. You just never saw us. *I* never saw *us*.

I, for one, have hungrily sought out that fuller picture and am working hard to contribute to showcasing it. However fraught and horrifying it often is, it's the one we live in. It's the one we must work with. It's the one we must change. But we can only reimagine the world if we see the one we're actually living in.

What Living in South Africa
Taught Me About Being
White in America

AS NOTED PREVIOUSLY, I GREW UP WHITE IN A TOWN largely full of white people (I believe 98 percent of the county I grew up in was white during the '80s). As a white, middle-class woman, I had the privilege to not care about the color of those around me. My color was the assumed default. As a child, my own whiteness—and my lack of exposure to current-day race relations—led me to believe that racism was some outmoded thing that no logical person would ever buy into. Because I was white, I had the privilege of being able to care—or not—about race, because I was of the "invisible" or assumed default in my hometown, my home state, and the media created and tailored for white people like me.

But like my starry-eyed belief that my gender also made no difference in the way I was perceived in the world, this was a short-lived notion that didn't last much past my teens. What I started to realize was that it didn't matter what I thought—there was already an institutionalized system in place, and it was the same system that ensured I grew up in a county that was 98 percent white.

When my great-grandmother died, my great-grandfather was

showing us some documents from around the time he bought his house in Portland, Oregon—around the '40s, I think. There was a marketing flyer for the neighborhood that basically said how it was a desirable place to live[1] because buses didn't go there (read: poor people) and "undesirable" people weren't allowed to live there (read: nonwhite people). The area had, of course, grown much more mixed over the years, and as far as my great-grandfather was concerned, this was the first step in its demise. I remember him grumbling over the paper, "Things were very different in this neighborhood then. Much better."

So of course I couldn't really see segregation, and how it worked, because I was so neatly cut off from people who were different from me. I lived in a place of invisible race because I was white. The people I saw every day were mostly white. At work, at school, at the mall—I just figured this was how it was. Of course race didn't matter and we were all the same, I told myself, but it's a lot easier to say that when all the people you see every day look the same way you do and are the same people making the laws and setting down the unwritten rules. And deciding where the white and nonwhite people live.

Because I was a white person growing up in white suburbia, it didn't really dawn on me how stiffly our country was still segregated until I spent a year and a half living in South Africa. In the United States, about 28 percent of our country is nonwhite now. In South Africa, over 80 percent of the country is nonwhite.

It does not escape my notice that having the means to go to graduate school overseas and live in Durban, South Africa, for nearly two years was its own kind of privilege, and that what I saw and experienced there was deeply informed by my own narrow upbringing.

I remember the first time I walked into a store in downtown Durban, just a few weeks after I arrived, and realized I was the only white person there. It was a startling moment of dissonance. I felt like I'd done something wrong, like maybe I wasn't supposed to be there. I realized I was twenty-two years old and had never in my life been the sole white person . . . hell, anywhere. And the knowledge of that, the striking realization that, in fact, the world I grew up in was a false one, that I had grown up under the false pretense that being white was somehow the norm, and that I had somehow picked up this strange illogical notion that the rest of the world was of course mostly white too, was absolutely shocking to me. We expect that we're smarter than that. That knowing something intellectually—of course the world is diverse and varied and wonderful and I had "known" that since I was a child—does not translate into real knowledge of that world until you experience it, was . . . really depressing, actually. Because I realized how many other white people in America had grown up just like me, in these false white rural and suburban ghettos where they had absolutely no idea of the actual composition of America. It's easier to uphold a lie when you segregate those who prove the lie wrong.

It didn't take long for me to adjust to my initial dissonance over being so white in a place where that wasn't the norm, of course. It became really normal for the world to not be monochrome. It was just life. Life was really vibrant when I lived in Durban. The people were incredibly nice, and the food was amazing. Sure, it wasn't all roses—the owners of my building hardly ever sprayed for bugs and often forgot to pay their water bill, and it was considered suicidal to go outside alone after dark—but I had a sliver of a view of the Indian Ocean and went to the beach whenever I wanted, and rent was the equivalent of $150 a month. I had a new normal. And that normal was—because of my race, my class, because of the country I came from—far better than many people were able to have in that city.

After living in Durban for eight months or so, I flew home to visit my family. I had a layover in the Minneapolis airport. I remember sitting there on a bench near the food court, scribbling in a notebook as people streamed by. After about an hour or so, I realized I felt deeply uncomfortable. Something felt very off. Very strange.

I looked up from my notebook and looked at the people streaming by . . . and realized what the source of my discomfort was.

Everyone was white.

Just as I'd done when I walked into that store where I was the only white person, I felt a moment of dissonance. Well, of course, I told myself—it's Minnesota. Of course everyone is white here. My brain neatly pushed that "normal" lever, where of course 99 percent white everything, everywhere is just "normal."

It wasn't until I went to the food court to get something to eat that I was reminded of the lie.

Because the people working in the food court? Were overwhelmingly nonwhite.

South Africa's segregation was easier for me to see because it was a foreign country. I could look at it as an outsider and point at all the flagrant abuses and government schemes that tried desperately to keep people separated. But seeing and experiencing that—and studying it deeply, which is what I was there to do—also allowed me to come back to my own country and finally, for the first time, see our own institutionalized segregation.[2] I could see how our government's programs and policies—even those from just ten or twenty or forty years before—had totally skewed the way we all experience the world, and though one's experience certainly relied on many factors including gender and wealth, race was a huge one.

I was reminded of this experience during a very laughable

postelection moment when I was viewing a video[3] from a Republican poll watcher in Aurora, Colorado. He was deeply concerned about the fact that the "racial mix" at the polling station he was at skewed far darker than "the mix of people at the mall." (!!) This, he said, was evidence of some kind of Democratic conspiracy to get more nonwhite people to this particular polling station.

What he failed to realize was that "these people" had been in Aurora all along—they simply didn't move in the same spaces he did. The only time he saw them was now, on Election Day, when they all had to come to the same place to vote. If he hadn't been a poll watcher, he likely would never have noticed them. Because that's privilege. Because that's having the ability to live in spaces that have been built to exclude others and give you a false sense of the world.

After living in Durban, I moved to Chicago and experienced that eerie train ride from the north side of Chicago to the south side, where the composition of people on the train changes so dramatically that it looks . . . planned. Because it was. Planned and enforced. Just as it had been in my great-grandfather's neighborhood in Portland, Oregon.

When I read a lot of golden age SF, I think about these guys who grew up in planned neighborhoods like my great-grandfather's, where people who were "different" from the false middle-class white "norm" were excluded. I think of television shows that still give us this narrow view of what "normal" is— so very white, so very male, with strict standards on body sizes and face shapes.

If this is the world you're fed every day, why wouldn't you replicate it? Of course the future is white and male and middle class. Of course the galactic empire is white and male and middle class. It is constructed that way. Just like our cities.

But no matter how many neighborhoods we gate off, or how many white faces we hand-select to deliver our media, it doesn't change the truth. It doesn't alter the math. Our world is a diverse and interesting one. It's not monochrome. To pretend otherwise is to live in a bubble of self-defeating lies and denial that serve no one and change nothing.

So when people tell me that including "so many" nonwhite characters in my fiction is "political" or that I'm trying to make some kind of "statement," I can't help countering with the fact that the "statement" made by every writer with a white mono-chrome world is also deeply political, even more so because it's based on a false sense of normal that's been carefully and sys-tematically constructed for hundreds of years in this country (and others).

I like to think that some folks slowly wake up to that lie, but until we succeed in desegregating the ways we live and work and actually start populating our media with an accurate representa-tion of what our world looks like, I figure we're still in for another fifty years of clunky—and increasingly ridiculous-looking—whitewashing.

As a creator, as a media-maker, I know I can choose to blindly perpetuate those myths, or help overturn them. But I couldn't make that choice until I stopped eating up the lie of what the world was really like.

It's About Ethics in Dating

GAMERGATE, WTF?

That's pretty much the reaction from anyone whenever I try to explain the organized trolling campaigns waged by a few hundred mostly young, mostly male gaming fans in 2014 and early 2015.

Never heard of Gamergate?

Let me explain.

No. There is too much. Let me sum up, because you know this story:

A young man and a young woman went out for a while. Eventually this young woman decided to call things off. They went back and forth about this for a time in the way that folks in their early twenties do, but eventually she was done with him and called it quits. The young man, instead of sitting in his room listening to Nine Inch Nails over and over again on repeat the way kids used to do, decided to post a screed online about all the horrible things—real and imagined—he believed his ex-girlfriend had done to him.[1] Most guys would and do simply get drunk with their friends around a fire and call the offending ex some names, and move on.

But no.

Too easy.

Too sane.

The whole of the gnashing underbelly of the internet picked the post up, and spurned ex-boyfriends everywhere rallied behind the guy's story. He'd hit a nerve. Many young men, taught by our culture to emote only anger and sarcasm, are ill-equipped when it comes to processing strong emotion. When you are promised the world and the world says it doesn't want you, you're left flailing and lashing out, and that's what these guys did.

In the churn of comments sections across the internet, someone decided the real problem here was that the young woman was a video game designer, and the man she was accused of sleeping with by her ex-boyfriend was a video game reviewer, and that this was some kind of breach of . . . ethics in gaming journalism. I'm unsure how this epiphany grew out of a spurned ex-boyfriend's explicit rant about his ex-girlfriend's supposed sexual exploits, but this is the internet. I suspect that it ties into the Fake Geek Girl fear. Surely the only reason this young woman slept with this young man was to get a positive review of her game, right?

Like I said: you know this story. You've heard it a thousand times a thousand. It is the woman journalist who must sleep with a source for a story. It's the woman who sleeps her way to the top. It's the harpy Jezebel, the Lady Macbeth, the scary sexual female who robs a man and, somehow, an entire industry of its manhood by daring to not have sex with people who want to have sex with her.

This kernel of an idea was quickly turned into #gamergate, a hashtag started to address this Evil Women in Gaming Problem that quickly became a smoke screen for notorious trolls and harassers of women in games to hide behind. By all counts, passionate Gamergate aficionados never made up more than three hundred to a thousand people, but when you're working online and you have a thousand people come at you, it feels like a freight train.

Suddenly women involved in all aspects of gaming, and some men, too, were fielding death and rape threats from folks associating themselves with the hashtag. One young man had a SWAT team called to his house. (This is a thing. Yes, called swatting. Why the FBI hasn't seriously shut the Gamergate folks down, I have no idea. Oh wait. Because they're still mostly going after women.[2]) Several women in gaming cancelled appearances and fled from their homes after getting very specific threats.

Gamergate was the organized, fully weaponized version of the stalker ex-boyfriend. It was like getting all the stalker ex-boyfriends together at a convention and giving them a hashtag to go vent about the wrongs done to them by all women everywhere.

I can only imagine what would have happened if my boyfriend from high school had had the internet as an outlet after our breakup. My friends told me he started calling around to all of them, after, spinning stories about how he was going to kill me and then drink bleach. He showed up once outside one of my college classes. He started dating one of my close friends and apparently told her about all the ways he was going to do me in, after telling her a great deal about our sexual history. During my next big breakup, at twenty-six, me and my ex both had blogs, and I told him it was fine if he wanted to talk about me but as a courtesy to not use my name.

"Don't name names for God's sake" became the polite way to deal with breakup and rejection, for me, in the internet age. But when you're posting someone's name to a forum with a long list of their personal and sexual failings, you aren't trying to "work through your feelings" or engender some kind of group therapy session or make a public service announcement about how other guys can avoid the same fate. You're there to hurt someone to try to make yourself feel better. You're out for revenge.

Gamergate became a revenge movement for every spurned ex-boyfriend and every guy who thought women's critique of and involvement in the gaming industry was somehow ruining his ability to play and enjoy the misogynist games he had come to know and love. They didn't want to hear that women like Anita Sarkeesian—who created a web series examining the portrayal of women in games—were doing so because they wanted to make the gaming industry better.

It's also no surprise that the backlash against women in gaming came at about the time that women reached parity in the gaming world. Women now make up about half of all gamers. Game makers can no longer pretend to ignore half of the people who play their games, and though every gaming audience is different, the reality is that there's more overlap between the people who play *Plants vs. Zombies* and *God of War* and *World of Warcraft* and *Mass Effect* than gamers and gaming companies would like to admit. (I play all those games.)

Many people I talk to about this organized hate campaign ask what it is about gaming that made this happen. When someone says this I wonder if they live in a different world than I do. Did they just hear what I said about weaponized stalker ex-boyfriends? We have created a culture that makes young men think it's okay to shame, harass, threaten, and ultimately rape and mutilate and kill young women because they are . . . upset. When men feel powerless and lash out we say, "Boys will be boys." I've been getting that sorry line as an excuse for bullying male behavior my whole life. Is it any wonder that when giving them some key, primarily female faces in gaming to hate and bully they don't act any differently than they did on the playground?

This dismissal of men's bad behavior happens when they are young, and continues even now as I listen to what law enforcement folks have to say to women harassed online. "Well, why don't you just get off the internet?" they say, or "Why don't you just stop posting stuff?" It's the exact same logic as the advice "If you don't want to be raped, just wear a long robe and stay in your house all day." These sorts of platitudes ignore and erase the reasons that men commit violence. They are violent because we as a society say it's all right, and it's a proper man thing to do, and there are few to no consequences for it. A restraining order is no big deal because everyone knows you were just served one because your ex-girlfriend is totally crazy, right?

It will surprise no one to learn that the young man whose angry screed began the campaign of harassment and abuse against dozens of women and men online was, as of this writing, dating again.[3] This is how the world works, after all. My ex is now married with three children. The world turns. Life goes on.

I have heard stories of the lives that my ex and his new family live, and I am incredibly gratified to have gotten away. People close to him tell me he has a concealed carry permit, and there's at least one bullet hole in his ceiling from when he got "really frustrated" with his wife. (If true, I'm even more glad I got away.) No doubt the new girlfriend of our spurned Gamergate instigator will be shocked, too, if one day the personal details of their relationship go up in some online screed, or when she ends up getting hurt, or stalked, or harassed. The next woman is always surprised when the rage turns to her, when she realizes that what is broken is the man at the keyboard, the man with the gun, the weaponized ex-boyfriend.

These are the men our society has made. What heartens me,

some days, is knowing that what is made can be remade. What is broken can be rebuilt. This isn't fate, or destiny. This is the end result of a series of stories that tells us women are things, and men deserve prizes. It's the end result of a bruised and formless masculinity so fragile and terrified and malformed by our society that the only thing those who wear it can do with their emotions is lash out in violence and rage in a terrible attempt at belonging.

I am tired of being asked, again and again, what women can do to save these men. What women can do to shield themselves from them. What women can do to protect themselves. I want a new conversation around what men can do to be better. What men can do to fix what is broken. What men can do to become human again, instead of wallowing in this monstrous stew of suffering and disappointment. I want to know what men can do to build a better world.

Hijacking the Hugo Awards

THE SCIENCE FICTION AND FANTASY LITERATURE WORLD might seem by its nature to be forward-thinking, but it hasn't been free from the kinds of culture wars embodied by 2014's Gamergate controversy[1]—a fact aptly illustrated by 2015's nominations for the genre's (arguably) most prestigious awards, the Hugos. The tastes of the voting audience for the Hugos, the attendees of the World Science Fiction Convention (or Worldcon), seem to have grown more diverse in recent years, and the selections have reflected that. In 2014 the awards were dominated by writers of color and women, myself included. So it was a surprise when a majority of voters woke up April 4 to a nomination slate almost exclusively overrun by novels, stories, and related fan efforts promoted by a small group of writers who claim the Hugos are turning into affirmative-action awards catering to left-wing ideologies. Their efforts to influence the voting process are led by a notorious right-wing novelist and internet personality who's best known for his desire to deny women the right to vote[2] and his firm belief that black people are "savages."[3]

When I won two awards last year, it seemed like an impossible achievement for me, because I knew the history of the Hugos. I knew they historically rewarded popular work set in the kinds of old, colonial, dudes-rule-everything universes that my work explicitly challenges. I never thought I'd be more than a fringe writer, but I also didn't believe science fiction was going to change, or that I'd be part of making that happen. I figured it would continue to tell the same old stories about the same old futures until the last of its readers died out, and that I'd be shouting for a more humanitarian future at the margins with others like me. But, like our wider culture, science fiction and fantasy fandom grew and shifted; and with it, our vision of the future changed, too.

Some aren't happy about that. Since 2013, one far-right novelist has led a small but vocal antiprogressive campaign called Sad Puppies (which has been accompanied by an even-worse campaign called Rabid Puppies) in an attempt to game the Hugos by mobilizing people to vote for its preferred choices. The secret of the awards is that they're actually very susceptible to manipulation—it costs just $40 for a supporting membership that includes voting rights. Low participation, paired with the sheer breadth of eligible work, means nominees can get onto the ballot with as few as fifty nominations. After failing to move the needle the first year, Sad Puppies organized around another slate of candidates and garnered an additional seventy or so votes in 2014 to edge a few of their chosen authors onto the ballot. The overall voting membership wasn't impressed with these choices, and awarded other work in every category. But in 2015, Sad Puppies—buoyed by support from the more extreme, Gamergate-affiliated campaign Rabid Puppies—managed to secure the extra votes needed to dominate the nominations. The result? They managed to push out those seeking to make the Hugos more representative of the diverse works within the genre.

As the writer and critic Abigail Nussbaum, herself a Hugo nominee, points out, schisms along political lines among science fiction and fantasy authors aren't new, nor is the subsequent ballot stuffing and logrolling in protest against awarding more literary work.[4] The author Samuel R. Delany wrote about his experience at the 1968 Nebula Awards, which are presented by the Science Fiction and Fantasy Writers of America.[5] When one of the presenters went on a long rant about how "pretentious literary nonsense" like Delany's and Roger Zelazny's was "abandoning the old values of good, solid, craftsmanlike storytelling," the room got very quiet. Delany won two awards that night—and received a standing ovation for his wins. Isaac Asimov, in a misguided attempt to cut the tension of the night, joked to Delany afterward that the reason they gave him the award was because "you're Negro," a remark Delany read as "a self-evidently tasteless absurdity" and a "standard male trope." But it was Delany himself who noted that the worst of the racist backlash in the science fiction community was yet to come.[6]

The genre has since grown dramatically, and in 2014, work by women and people of color from a diverse range of publishers swept the Nebula Awards in addition to dominating the Hugos. So why are so many fringe groups escalating their protests in gaming, in comics, and in the science fiction community? Why should it matter that there was a bloc vote led in large part by a group whose most vociferous leader wants to disenfranchise entire groups of people?

The truth is that our wars of words and narrative matter, especially those that tell us what sorts of possible futures we can build—and groups like Gamergate, the Sad Puppies, and their angrier companion movement the Rabid Puppies understand this. The author Ursula K. Le Guin said it best in her National Book Award acceptance speech:

We live in capitalism. Its power seems inescapable. So did the divine right of kings. Any human power can be resisted and changed by human beings. Resistance and change often begin in art, and very often in our art—the art of words.

The demographics of the United States are shifting (by 2050, people of color will outnumber Caucasians),[7] and young people's views are becoming increasingly liberal (even 61 percent of young Republicans favor same-sex marriage).[8] The effects of this are being felt across all aspects of our public life. The media being consumed now is different than that preferred by the dominant culture of the 1990s, let alone the 1950s, and there's undeniably a greater appetite for progressive stories.

So it's no coincidence that many of the people bloc-voting these awards are the same ones sending death threats to women and people of color,[9] sending SWAT teams to the addresses of critics,[10] and hijacking accounts and identities to try to silence those creating more inclusive stories. Suppressing the recognition that comes from winning awards also serves to silence the futures being written—how many works will we *not* see this year reprinted in the awards lists in major publications?

Historically, science fiction and fantasy literature is no stranger to controversy, but it has learned how to adapt and endure. Some of the most exciting conversations about power and resistance are happening in the field, and it's these books and their creators that are increasingly the starting point for original television shows and movies that weave themselves into wider cultural narratives, from Hiroshi Sakurazaka's *All You Need Is Kill* (the basis for the film *Edge of Tomorrow*) to James S. A. Corey's new *Expanse* series on Syfy with its incredibly diverse cast. Chuck Wendig's *Blackbirds* adaptation on Starz features a tough, trash-talking heroine. The science fiction authors Tananarive Due and Steven

Barnes crowdfunded a short zombie film starring Frankie Faison of *The Wire*.

G. Willow Wilson and Genevieve Valentine are two science fiction authors among those writing reboots of the wildly popular Ms. Marvel (now in its seventh printing) and Catwoman comics, reimagining Ms. Marvel as a young Muslim woman and addressing Catwoman's bisexuality directly. Even Ann Leckie's gender-bending space opera *Ancillary Justice*, which dominated the field's awards in 2014, has been optioned for film. And these names and titles only represent a fraction of this growing movement. The reality is that much of the stuff you see in film, television, comics, and children's cartoons got its start inside the inspired, disruptive halls of science fiction and fantasy literature.

It's lucky for us—writers, readers, and everyone else—that the fiction of the future is much more difficult to game than an awards ballot.

In truth, the future that groups like Gamergate and the Sad and Rabid Puppies are arguing so vehemently against is already here.

Dear SFWA Writers:
Let's Chat About Censorship
and Bullying

THE SFWA, OR SCIENCE FICTION AND FANTASY WRITERS of America, has gone through a number of growing pains over the years. This came to a head from 2011 to 2014. Under the new leadership of John Scalzi, Mary Robinette Kowal, and Rachel Swirsky—and later, Steven Gould—the organization began to put a greater emphasis on industry professionalism, which necessitated a dramatic change in the way the organization's communications were run. With this team at the helm, there was significant blowback from industry professionals and fans who expected greater change and weren't getting it. A woman-in-chain-mail-bikini cover for one issue of *The Bulletin*—the organization's industry magazine—in which two former members of the organization waxed on about the attractiveness of "lady editors" back in the day drew fire. When the next issue came out with a response from the two men that basically likened those who complained to Nazis and thought police, several members resigned in protest.[1]

What fascinated me was the complete cluelessness of those whose actions drew the ire of the internet. On some level, sure, I get it: the world used to agree with you. You used to be able to say things like, "I really like those lady writers in this industry, especially in swimsuits!" and your fellow writers, editors, agents, and other assorted colleagues would all wink and grin and agree with you, and Asimov would go around pinching women's asses, and it was so cool! So cool that he could just sexually assault women all the time! You used to be able to say, "Black people are fine. As long as they are clean and don't live in my neighborhood," and your friends and colleagues would wink and grin and agree with you. You'd say, "Gay men are gay because they were abused, and all lesbians are really bisexual and just need the love of a good man," and hey, it was okay, because no one disagreed with you.

You came to believe that what you believed and what you said were true. It was the narrative. You felt happy and self-important about it, because you got it. Sure, you were tolerant. You accepted everyone! You just told it like it was. You stated your opinion. Maybe sometimes people said stuff like, "Well, maybe that's kind of racist," but you just waved your hand and bellowed, "I'm not a racist!" and then stopped inviting them to parties. Problem solved.

In fact, everyone you knew agreed with you when you said these things, or, if they didn't agree, they grinned and winked and gritted their teeth instead. In fact, a lot more of them likely gritted their teeth and bore it than you could ever imagine. But by stating your opinion without getting disagreement or pushback, a funny thing happened. You started to believe that your narrative was the only narrative. That your opinion was the sound one. The only one. Absolute, untouchable truth.

Well, welcome to the future. And the internet, where everybody, even those underprivileged nobodies you never had to listen to before, has a chance to be heard.

Surprise. Not everybody agrees with you. In fact, many have not agreed with you for a long, long time, and because you lived such an insulated life, only talking on forums with the same old people, about the same old things, you started to believe that nobody disagreed with you. You'd never even experienced what it was like to have the very people you were denigrating say to you, out loud, "You've gravely disrespected me." And if they did, they were just humorless bitches, and nobody wanted to work with them anyway, and they weren't in any power to impact your career, being little bitches and all, so you didn't pay any real attention.

That was your privilege.

Worse, because you likely occupied a place of power in the hierarchy of the publishing industry, having a lot of books under your belt and a lot of contacts, nobody publicly disagreed with you. They feared the repercussions. They knew that you and your little groups of established pros could ruin their careers. They knew you'd call them mad, humorless, and not somebody fun to be around or do business with. So they sucked it up. They smiled. They played along. They drank whisky and made fun of other women with you. You may not even have realized it. Because that was your privilege.

In order to do business in a biased, sexist, racist, fucked-up industry, you have to plaster on your smile and nod when people say the most outrageously disrespectful, fucked-up things about you and people like you. When these dudes tell you it's nice that you write novels but it sure would be nice if you had better tits so they could put you in bikini armor and slap you on the cover of their industry magazine for their buddies to leer at, you just smile, ha-ha isn't that funny and get them another beer because you're desperate to be in their upcoming anthology. Yes, I have a sense of humor! Please don't boot me from this organization! I want to make this my career, so I will smile at every disrespectful, sexist thing you say and pretend it's totally hilarious! Because this is what I've been trained to do. It's how I get ahead. It's the only way.

I know this from experience. My blog had a lot more fucking teeth before I started publishing books.

And while these women or people of color are smiling at you they're actively writing their own stories, and growing their own audiences, and hoping for the day when everybody finally stands up and says, "You know, actually, disrespecting half your colleagues and reducing them to a pair of tits or collection of bigoted stereotypes isn't okay."

"But why?" you might ask. "Why'd people grin and bear it?" Folks, we have to grin and bear it in an organization where forty-eight people voted for an organizational president who says women shouldn't be allowed to vote.[2] In my own industry. In the one that pays me to write books. Forty-eight people were happy to publicly endorse turning me into a nonhuman. How many more were sympathetic to this? How many that I don't know about?

I'm not immune to criticism on the internet. I'm from a privileged population, too. I'm white, and American, and middle class. I am adept at getting yelled at by all sorts of people. I've had people angry with me about racist and homophobic tropes they identified in my books, people brave enough to stand up and say, "You know what? This thing you did here? Did you see that? It's not okay. It hurt."

And you know what? That is not censorship. That is brave.

Let me tell you something about censorship and bullying. Because I've experienced that—what that *really* is—too. Bullying censorship is death threats and sexual threats. Endless ones. Endless on a scale you cannot even imagine.[3] It's coordinated attacks from people who really would rather you were dead than that you keep talking. Dead and raped, preferably.

People get angry. Nobody has to agree with you anymore. Nobody is afraid of you anymore. I know this may come as a massive shock to folks used to a position of power, insulated by groups of people who are happy to stroke their egos and soothe their souls. Truth be told, many of these people don't even feel like they're in power. I know I never do. But it's time to face the fact that people disagree with you, and that's their right.

I have dealt with people actually trying to silence me from the moment I posted my first blog post in 2004. And because of that, I find myself deeply offended to hear you claim that having people ask that an industry magazine be more respectful of all its members, not just the dudes, is equivalent to a massive witch hunt meant to emasculate you. Your insistence that you're being bullied by Nazis trivializes the actual bullying, death threats, and sexual threats people get in this industry simply for asking to be treated like human beings.

Here are some tips on how to take criticism, real criticism, on the internet, from somebody who has been dealing with both sides of this for a decade:

Start actually listening. For once in your privileged life, listen. Listen. Because if I punched you, and you said, "Gosh, that really hurt," and I said, "YOU ARE FUCKING CENSORING ME YOU FUCKING COMMUNIST," you'd think I was insane.

Listen. Do better. Understand privilege and power. Understand why people didn't speak up before. Why you didn't hear it before. If you hit somebody, and you really didn't mean to, would you say, "Well, it's your fault for having tits"? Or would you say, "I'm so sorry I hit you. That wasn't my intention. I will actively work to not hit you in the future."

I know what somebody who was genuinely interested in open, honest, respectful dialogue with people they considered humans and colleagues would do.

With Great Power Comes Great Responsibility: On Empathy and the Power of Privilege

I HAD THE QUESTIONABLE DELIGHT OF HANGING OUT WITH a three-year-old one week, and at some point, when I hauled off his pants so he could go "pee-pee in the potty," he proceeded to sit on said toilet for a solid five minutes having an argument with me because I'd said "Hey!" when he tried to hit his mother.

"You YELLED at me!" he yelled. "We don't yell in this house."

"We don't hit our mom, either."

"We don't YELL. You HURT my FEELINGS."

At some point, this child will understand the difference between a feeling of guilt for being called out when he does something bad and actual hurt feelings, but today is not that day.

"And you hurt your mom's feelings," I said. "You don't hit your mom."

"We don't YELL IN THIS HOUSE."

"We don't hit our mother."

About this time, I realized I was standing in a bathroom arguing with a half-naked three-year-old child, and I needed to cut my losses and walk away, because I was the adult. I would never convince him that his feeling of guilt was not as serious as him having almost hit his mother; I'd get stuck in a toddler logic loop. Because what one almost does to someone one sees as so far outside the self when one is three is not something that's ever going to compute. What's going to register is YOU hurt MY feelings.

What almost happened to his mom is moot.

I was reminded of this particular exchange when listening to folks rage—both on Twitter and in mainstream media—about what idiots folks in fandom were for rising up in rage against having media personality Jonathan Ross host the Hugo Awards.[1] Ross, like many comedians, was known to have made sexist and other uncomfortable, off-color jokes. Many in the science fiction and fantasy community reacted with outrage, expressing fears that he would denigrate them in their own space. After just eight hours of internet commentary on the decision, Ross resigned from the gig, and writer Neil Gaiman wrote a post expressing his disappointment with fans and industry professionals for how they communicated their anger at Ross's appointment. A schism opened up between fans and pros who thought having Ross would have been a boon to the award, and those who felt his presence would be contentious and inappropriate. Interestingly, in the aftermath of this affair, the way the story was constructed by many in the popular media (aside from Laurie Penny) was that Ross—a media professional with a following of over three million—had been "bullied" by ungrateful science fiction fans into resigning.

Because in all the rage about how fandom must be full of crazy idiots who no longer have a Great White Hope to Save Their Genre from Obscurity, what nobody seemed to remember was that the actual pushback on Twitter was not raised fists to hit him, but expressions of fear that Ross was going to hit their mom. It was the internet yelling, "HEY!" and asking for reassurance that they wouldn't be diminished, spat on, ridiculed, or raged at in their own house.[2]

In fact, folks like Farah Mendlesohn spoke up pretty clearly about this early on, before the announcement of Ross's hosting was made public (her post about resigning her committee position over the issue has since been made private), and Seanan McGuire bravely stated her fears point-blank on Twitter—fears which, if I were a Hugo nominee and attendee, I would also share. Farah and Seanan are both people I respect highly, and I take their concerns seriously. But others did not. So there was no accompanying statement, no reassurance from either Ross or those who chose him, just "Here he is. YOU SHOULD BE GRATEFUL YOU UNWASHED MASSES."

And in response, two highly respected women's concerns were shrugged off like "Bitches must be crazy."

When you play the "Bitches must be crazy" card, the internet won't be far behind you, my friends.

I'm a fat nerd. I've been bullied my whole life. When the kids in school stopped, there was the wider world out there to tell me I was too big, too loud, too smart, too brash. I got used to being hit. I saw it happen all the time.

What we want when we say "HEY!" to someone—and someone, in this case, who has vastly more power than we do—is reassurance. We're looking for an explanation, a statement, that this person gets where we're coming from, and despite our fears, isn't going to raise his fist to hit us. This is not rocket science. It's not a tough thing to figure out if you apply a little empathy.

EMPATHY, JOURNALISTS. Try it sometime.

Sadly, empathy is the one thing that a lot of the mainstream pieces covering the incident seemed to ignore. I haven't seen one piece that actually took the concerns of the community seriously. Instead of a concert of concerned, formerly bullied geeks looking for reassurance, it was a "Twitter mob" with pitchforks and torches banging on some rich dude's door, baying for blood.

I realize that angry Twitter mob[2] makes for a more compelling clickbait story, but casting Jay Leno, or Howard Stern, or the cast of *SNL* as victim because a few dozen or a few hundred people on Twitter said, "HEY DON'T HIT ME I'M AFRAID YOU'LL HIT ME THE WAY YOU DID PERSON X" would be absurd, and we'd call it out as such. When did the privileged become victims? Did somebody send the dude a rape threat? Did he have to get a restraining order against somebody on Twitter? Because these are things that happen to the people who spoke up, these are things that happen to us all the time, and are probably happening to many of the women who said, "HEY I'M AFRAID YOU'LL HIT ME!" either to or about Ross publicly. And unlike the rich with big voices, we don't have as many resources we can set in motion to protect ourselves when those threats do come in.

We speak out because we are brave, not because we're baying for blood. We speak out because we're tired of being hit, and we need to know that if you're coming into our house, you're not going to act like an asshole. We went to school with that dude. We deal with that dude on the internet every day.

We are fucking tired of that dude.

So instead of snarking back at people on Twitter and calling them nut jobs and invoking Neil Gaiman's name as a ward of protection, it would have behooved the privileged person to stand back and say, "Hey. Wow. I'm so sorry! I didn't realize so many of you had that impression. Let me assure you that I love and support this community and I take this gig seriously. I respect and love every single one of you and please be assured I'll be respectful and welcoming, just as I hope you will be respectful and welcoming to me as a host."

Yeah, that's a tough thing to do when you're being yelled at. Trust me. I've been there. But it's the adult thing to do. It's the thing the person with the most power needs the guts to be able to do. It comes with the job.

Because when somebody says, "I'm afraid you'll hit me," and you say, "FUCK YOU! WHY WOULD I HIT YOU? YOU THINK I'M A MONSTER OR SOMETHING, YOU FUCKING IDIOT!" it is going to achieve exactly the opposite impression of what you purport to intend.

The truth of the matter is that my saying "HEY!" prevented the three-year-old from hitting his mom. Oh, you can say all you like that maybe he was just raising his arm to hit her and wouldn't have carried through, but I'd seen it before. I knew I'd see it again. And somebody needed to say "HEY!" and prevent it.

Yes, I raised my voice. And to a self-involved toddler, raising one's voice, especially when everyone tells you not to, can seem like the gravest of crimes. But the truth of the matter is that a few dozen people yelling "HEY!" on the internet at a public figure with a global following and three million Twitter followers is even less of a threat or mob or grave insult than an adult raising their voice to a toddler. The person with the privilege is the public figure.

In this case, that's not angry fans or even pros on Twitter who are fearful of being hit, and who express that in a reasonable, passionate way.

It's the public figure with the power to hit.

And if the public figure can't show empathy, or respond cordially, as befitting their place of power, but instead snarks at people on Twitter and walks off in a huff without even trying, I can't help wondering if they were really such a good fit in the first place.

So please stop sharing those annoying articles that call bullied nerds a bunch of idiots who want to keep their genre in the ghetto. They don't. What they want is to feel they're marginally more safe among their people than they are in the wider world, even if, as recent sexist meltdowns have shown us, that's not really true. We want to believe it. We want to believe things are getting better. We've been hit before, and when we see a raised fist now—or even a potential raised fist—we react in the way that survivors do, with caution that from the outside, to those without empathy, may look nuts, but to us is born out of sheer self-preservation.

Nobody likes how the Ross thing went down. But let's not heap this on Twitter's shoulders, but on the shoulders of those with the most privilege, who should have stepped back, applied empathy, and responded accordingly.

I'll remind folks that it wasn't long ago when a pretty well-known writer got into it on Twitter for a tweet taken out of context, and after a harrowing beginning, apologized publicly and graciously and then individually to each person who may have felt harmed by the exchange.[3]

That's how people with perceived power and privilege act when the shit goes down: they grit their teeth and bear it, with grace.

I've done it myself, though I often feel powerless, because it's not my own perceived power that matters. It's the power other people give me.

When a perceived or assumed harm has been done, one needs to first express remorse about the situation and the pain caused. These sorts of statements generally begin with "I'm sorry . . ." or "I apologize . . ." Next, one must admit to one's behavior. In this case, it was past behavior that many Hugo attendees thought would be carried over into Ross's hosting of this event. The third step is to make amends—to reach out to those who have been harmed by one's behavior in the past and make things right. And finally, one must reassure one's audience that that behavior won't happen again.

With great power comes great responsibility. You must prove

that you know what to do with it. The mob isn't always out wailing for blood. Sometimes it's just begging you to prove them
wrong and reassure them that their fears are unfounded. How
we choose to engage or not with real fear, and real criticism, as
opposed to trolling, says a lot about us as human beings—and
creators.

Rage Doesn't Exist in a Vacuum

I ONCE STOOD AT A BUS STOP IN DURBAN WHILE TWO young, drunk men murmured sexually explicit threats and promises to a young woman standing next to me. It was just the four of us—the woman being threatened, me, and the two perpetrators.

South Africa is not the world's safest place, though with how often folks pull out guns to solve disagreements in the United States—legally!—now, I'd argue it's not so safe here, either. In any event, I kept my mouth shut. After all, they weren't threatening her with an actual weapon. They were just talking about all the sexual things they wanted to do to her.

It didn't concern *me*.

I didn't want to get knifed, or attacked, or threatened in kind. Who wants that?

But after a few minutes, when they didn't seem to tire of their threats, but instead kept at it, I finally lost my shit.

It was a fantastic losing-of-the-shit, because I'd spent the last six months hurrying back to my flat before dark, being told by every well-meaning person I knew that there were evil men waiting to rape, mutilate, and murder me—maybe not even in that order!—even in broad daylight. I had one guy in a car slow down once on a sunny Sunday afternoon on the hill just outside the university where I was walking alone, who told me I'd best not walk alone, and best get inside, because people were likely to jump out of the woods and haul me off to the terrible fate all young white girls traveling abroad are assumed to inhabit, eventually.

I'd spent some time getting catcalled, yelled at, and solicited, though most folks in Durban were in fact quite lovely. In truth, I received far more direct threats and harassment as a young woman living in Chicago than I did in Durban.

But that's a subject for another time.

To an outsider seeing my screaming meltdown at these two men—in which I raved and shouted and told them how they were utter assholes for harassing us, and they should fuck off, and who the fuck did they think they were—this might have seemed like the raving of some unhinged person. After all, from afar, all you see is two guys at a bus stop talking to a woman who seems deeply uncomfortable. But my rage, my "sudden" outburst, was actually the venting of six full months of increasing dread and terror inflicted on me not even so much by actual bad people, but people ostensibly concerned for my safety, whose admonitions that I "stay inside" and watch my back, and be careful—and who would then go on to talk about who'd been raped, shot, stabbed, or mugged that week—had really started to get to me. It was a rage at the entire situation, at being expected to shut the fuck up and go inside all the time because I was a young woman. It was rage at the idea that the threat of violence so clearly worked to keep people in line.

After I raged for a few minutes, the guys milled about for a bit, confused, and finally wandered off. When they did, the young woman next to me breathed a sigh of relief and said, "Thank you so much. I was afraid to say something, because I was afraid they'd knife me or something."

When the internet loses its shit over what, to many, looks like a single, insignificant incident unrelated to anything else, it's easy to say they're fucking nuts. They're raging over some perceived slight that's been blown waaaaay out of proportion. That, in truth, is the easier narrative. There's a reason folks say things like "Women are crazy" to explain away some perceived hurt or slight, because it's easier than thinking through why that rage makes one so uncomfortable (often because one is complicit in acts that contribute to that rage in some way by perpetuating both sexism and the belittling of women's voices). It's easier to say people are crazy than to try to figure out why.

Especially when you're in a place where it's never your butt getting hurt.[1]

Internet rage is almost never a one-off.[2] It happens in a continuum. It's seen as one more event in a long line of connected events.

About ten years ago, some dude blogger with a big following would ask, about every six months, "Where are all the women bloggers? I don't read any women bloggers. So women must not blog!"

And the feminist blogosphere would fall on him.

Every. Six. Months.

We'd clog up his blog comments with our voices. We'd link to other women's blogs. We'd point out that the reason he never saw women was because it was easier to not see them. It was easier to link to the dudes that he knew.

You don't see people you don't listen to.

That went on for a couple of years. At some point, after *Wonkette* got big and Amanda Marcotte got tapped to do social media outreach for a major political candidate, these conversations

stopped. (Now it's "here are all the people you should be following on Twitter" lists that don't have a single person of color on
them, even though people of color make up over 40 percent of
Twitter users and generate the majority of tweets and some of
the biggest online memes and movements have originated with
influential folks on that end. Same shit, different pocket.)

We got all sorts of pushback on this, about how we should be
more "civil" and "settle down." We got told we were "overreact-
ing." We were being "pushy bitches" and "making something out
of nothing."

But the truth was that unless we made a big fucking stink,
people went back to the status quo.

Folks will always, always, always go back to the comfortable
status quo, with its silent voices and lack of conflict, if you give
them the chance.

"Settle the fuck down, you got your way" also doesn't work
after a fight is over, because though dudes may go, "Yeah, we get
it, women blog," unless you're on it like a fucking train wreck,
you'll have the conversation again six months later.

They forget. They start rewriting the narrative.[3]

Calls for civility,[4] as well-intentioned as they may be, smack
to me of folks telling me I should have swallowed my tongue at
the bus stop. After all, it's not as if the men were physically harm-
ing the young woman. And I should have held my tongue when
people said women don't blog, because obviously if I wrote well
enough, and shut up enough, and acted demure enough, people
would just magically notice me, right?

Clearly, y'all have no idea how this works.

Oh. Wait. You do.

If I shut the fuck up, then all the people you quote, all the
people who write the postnarrative, the big pieces that folks look
back on to create the history and narrative of an event, even

a successful one, will be made by the powerful, influential people who believe their hurt feelings at being called out as problematic somehow outweigh the concerns of an entire community of folks with no media pull and no platform whose voices have been marginalized their whole lives and who are now being reduced to a crazy, screaming, angry mob acting up out of nowhere instead of a passionate community of folks reacting to an event they see as existing on a problematic continuum.

We have a strange habit of falling back on "civility," as if every social movement was entirely civil. Like unions didn't bust up on scabs. Like Nelson Mandela didn't blow shit up.[5] Like MLK would tell us all to shut the fuck up,[6] and women never chained themselves to the fences in city squares, stormed political buildings, or committed acts of arson and violence in an effort to achieve suffrage.

Surprise!

My specialization is in the history of revolutionary movements, and let me tell you, folks—being nice and holding hands didn't get shit done. Or sure, it was one tactic. But never the *only* tactic. I wish a nice circle-jerk got shit done as much as the next person, but if it were so, history would look much, much different.

Change is messy. It's angry. It's uncomfortable. It's full of angry people saying angry things, because they've been disrespected and forgotten again and again and again and again, and they're tired of being fucking nice because it makes you uncomfortable if they act in any way that is not deferential or subservient to you and your worldview.

I'm sorry if we've interrupted your latest Kickstarter, or pin-up calendar, or the purchase of your million-dollar estate in California, and you're throwing all your Hugo pins into Mount Doom in the hopes it will shame us into silence.

That must be really, really tough.

I'm sympathetic; I really am. Because I too know what it is to be comfortable and safe and pretend everything's fine. I'm white. My parents aren't poor, and I make decent money now. I get how annoying it can be, to get called out on that, and to have to listen to people who have problems you don't. Real fucking problems and issues that exist on a continuum of shame, disrespect, and forced subservience they've had to deal with their whole lives.

For a community of folks who grew up reading comic books and farmers-who-become-heroes, we sure do balk when we suddenly go from farm boy to hero. Because that's a heavy fucking responsibility, and it's easier to pretend you're still mewling Peter Parker, complaining about how no girl will fuck you. You may not feel like you have power or influence, but you do—as do I.

There are a few things we can do when we have power and influence.

We can take our toys and go home.

Or we can get the fuck up and fight for the people who are continually shit on, and act like a fucking hero would act.

I know which I'd rather do.

Why I'm Not Afraid of the Internet

MY GRANDMOTHER GREW UP IN NAZI-OCCUPIED FRANCE. When she was nineteen, she and her friends found a Nazi boot containing a severed human leg while walking along the river. For every Nazi the French killed, the Nazis would kill ten French citizens. So how many would the Nazis kill, my grandmother thought, for a severed leg? She and her friends huffed the boot and its fleshy occupant back into the river and spent the next month waiting to hear how many of them would be shot in the street.

There's nothing I experience online that can rival what my grandmother went through. I've been living loudly online for ten years, getting my fair share of abuse and threats, but—vastly more often—grateful notes for having the courage to speak boldly. My grandmother's stories gave me a great deal of perspective—both on life and on the tactics of terror, and how silence serves a darker future. Unchecked hate can be insidious, and can creep up and consume whole swaths of a culture before they even know what's happening. Which is why you have to keep speaking, and fighting for a better future.

I also have a unique perspective on life shared by many

survivors of near-death experiences. When I came to in the ICU when I was twenty-six after nearly two days in a coma, the doctor told me that if they'd hauled me in ten years before I'd be dead. They simply wouldn't have had the equipment to save me. Having a chronic illness like mine where you have to take medication multiple times a day in order to survive means death is always one miscalculation or mix-up away. Death hugs you close every day, whispering a siren song far more terrifying than any internet mob.

When I talk about this online, I get a lot of pushback from people who think I don't believe that internet threats are serious, that I don't think there are people fully capable and enabled by the misogyny of our society to act on those threats. Quite the contrary. I believe it wholeheartedly.

There are men everywhere who feel that being rejected by women entitles them to murder those women. There are men who will single out you, as a public figure, for embodying everything they feel is wrong with women. You are the reason women laugh at them or won't have sex with them, or you are the reason their girlfriend broke up with them. One of the things Gamergate taught us is just how far men are willing to go to shame and threaten the women who hurt their feelings, and how many other men think that's all right. I know that stalker boyfriend who refuses to believe it's over. And all those stalker boyfriends and potential stalker boyfriends have found each other on the internet, and they are looking for targets.

I hear people say, more and more these days, that they are fearful to say anything online. Fearful to have an opinion or a position that might be seen as "controversial," even if it's, you know, *truthful*. And that really bothers me.

The reality is that you're more likely to get killed by a family member or an ex-boyfriend than by a stranger online. According to my friends, my ex-boyfriend called them up and described to them all the new and inventive ways he had come up with to kill me and then himself. He showed up outside my college classes and sent me horrifying emails. I know that's horrifically sad, but it's true. It's the society we live in. Our fear of strangers has always been a stalking horse for the real threat, and that's the people closest to us: our friends, our family, our lovers. Our discussions about the dangers of online discourse make the strangers of the internet into some kind of bogeyman, when in fact they are all simply specters of a broken and systematically misogynist world.

My grandmother often carried around a bullet that she said came from two planes that were in a dogfight overhead. She said you could tell which planes were German and which were American by the sound of the engines. A stray bullet from the dogfight grazed the side of her head and embedded itself in the wall behind her. If we asked, she would lift up a hank of hair and show us the long scar. She dug out the bullet and kept it with her all through her long journey from France to the United States. When we asked her why, she said it was because, as a lifelong Catholic, she believed that it meant God had spared her for greater things. She was meant to endure. She was meant to live.

So when you ask me if I'm afraid of the internet, and the self-entitled wanker of the day gaming awards, or the five hundred people who yell at me on Twitter, or some internet personality having a meltdown in my general direction, I think of my grandmother throwing that severed leg back into the river, and I say, "You're kidding, right?"

There's a future I'm meant to be a part of. We are building it one narrative at a time.

Yes, change is incredibly terrifying, and there will be pushback and threats and dudes on the internet loudly declaring that you are a big vagina as if that is the worst possible thing a human being can be. But this is not yet Nazi-occupied France, my friends.

Are there ramifications for speaking up? Sure. Muting people can get tedious. But you're still more likely to be hit by a bus than shivved by a sobbing internet mob.

We are made of tougher stuff than we can ever imagine.

We Have Always Fought: Challenging the "Women, Cattle, and Slaves" Narrative

I'M GOING TO TELL YOU A STORY ABOUT LLAMAS. IT WILL be like every other story you've ever heard about llamas: how they are covered in fine scales; how they eat their young if not raised properly; and how, at the end of their lives, they hurl themselves—lemming-like—over cliffs to drown in the surging sea. They are, at heart, sea creatures, birthed from the sea, married to it like the fishing people who make their livelihood there.

Every story you hear about llamas is the same. You see it in books: the poor doomed baby llama getting chomped up by its intemperate parent. On television: the massive tide of scaly llamas falling in a great, majestic herd into the sea below. In the movies: badass llamas smoking cigars and painting their scales in jungle camouflage.

Because you've seen this story so many times, because you already know the nature and history of llamas, it sometimes shocks you, of course, to see a llama outside of these media spaces. The llamas you see don't have scales. So you doubt what you see, and you joke with your friends about "those scaly llamas" and they laugh and say, "Yes, llamas sure are scaly!" and you forget your actual experience.

What you remember is the llama you saw who had mange, which sort of looked scaly, after a while, and that one llama who was sort of aggressive toward a baby llama, like maybe it was going to eat it. So you forget the llamas that don't fit the narrative you saw in films, books, television—the ones you heard about in the stories—and you remember the ones that exhibited the behavior the stories talk about. Suddenly, all the llamas you remember fit the narrative you see and hear every day from those around you. You make jokes about it with your friends. You feel like you've won something. You're not crazy. You think just like everyone else.

And then there came a day when you started writing about your own llamas. Unsurprisingly, you didn't choose to write about the soft, downy, noncannibalistic ones you actually met, because you knew no one would find those "realistic." You plucked out the llamas from the stories. You created cannibal llamas with a death wish, their scales matted in paint.

It's easier to tell the same stories everyone else does. There's no particular shame in it.

It's just that it's lazy, which is just about the worst possible thing a spec fic writer can be.

Oh, and it's not *true*.

As somebody with more than a passing knowledge of history, I'm passionately interested in truth: truth is something that happens whether or not we see it, or believe it, or write about it. Truth just is. We can call it something else, or pretend it didn't happen, but its repercussions live with us, whether we choose to remember and acknowledge it or not.

When I sat down with one of my senior professors in Durban, South Africa, to talk about my master's thesis, he asked me why I wanted to write about women resistance fighters.

"Because women made up twenty percent of the ANC's militant wing!" I gushed. "Twenty percent! When I found that out I couldn't believe it. And you know—women have never been part of fighting forces—"

He interrupted me. "Women have always fought," he said.

"What?" I said.

"Women have always fought," he said. "Shaka Zulu had an all-female force of fighters. Women have been part of every resistance movement. Women dressed as men and went to war, went to sea, and participated actively in combat for as long as there have been people."

I had no idea what to say to this. I had been nurtured in the U.S. school system on a steady diet of the Great Men theory of history. History was full of Great Men. I had to take separate women's history courses just to learn about what women were doing while all the men were killing each other. It turned out many of them were governing countries and figuring out rather effective methods of birth control that had sweeping ramifications on the makeup of particular states, especially Greece and Rome.

Half the world is full of women, but it's rare to hear a narrative that doesn't speak of women as the people who have things done to them instead of the people who do things. More often, women are talked about as a man's daughter. A man's wife.

I just watched a reality TV show about Alaska bush pilots where all of the pilots get these little intros about their families and passions, but the single female pilot is given the one-line "Pilot X's girlfriend." It wasn't until they broke up, in season two, that she got her own intro. Turns out she's been in Alaska four times longer than the other pilot and hunts, fishes, and climbs ice walls, in addition to being an ace pilot.

But the narrative was "cannibalistic llama," and our eyes glazed over, and we stopped seeing her as anything else.

* * *

Language is a powerful thing, and it changes the way we view ourselves, and other people, in delightful and horrifying ways. Anyone with any knowledge of the military, or who pays attention to how the media talks about war, has likely caught on to this.

We don't kill "people." We kill "targets." (Or japs or gooks or ragheads.) We don't kill "fifteen-year-old boys" but "enemy combatants." (Yes, every boy fifteen and over killed in drone strikes now is automatically listed as an enemy combatant. Not a boy. Not a child.)

And when we talk about "people" we don't really mean "men and women." We mean "people and female people." We talk about "American Novelists" and "American Women Novelists."[1] We talk about "Teenage Coders" and "Lady Teenage Coders."[2]

And when we talk about war, we talk about soldiers and *female* soldiers.

Because this is the way we talk, when we talk about history and use the word "soldiers" it immediately erases any women doing the fighting. Which is why it comes as no surprise that the folks excavating Viking graves didn't bother to check whether the graves they dug up were male or female. They were graves with swords in them. Swords are for *soldiers*. Soldiers are *men*.

It was years before they thought to even check the actual bones of the skeletons instead of just saying "Sword means dude!" and realized their mistake.[3]

Women fought too.

In fact, women did all sorts of things we think they didn't do. In the Middle Ages, they were doctors and sheriffs.[4] In Greece they were . . . [5] Let's just put it this way: if you think there's a thing—anything—women didn't do in the past, you're wrong. Women—now and then—even made a habit of peeing standing up. They wore dildos. So even things the funny-ha-ha folks immediately raise a hand to say, like, "It's impossible women did

X!" Well. They did it. Intersex women and trans women, too, have fought and died, often misgendered and forgotten, in the ranks of history. And let us remember, when we speak about women and men as if these are immutable, somehow "historical" categories, that there are those who have always lived and fought in the seams between things.

But none of those things fit our narrative. What we want to talk about are women in one capacity: their capacity as wife, mother, sister, daughter to a man. I see this in fiction all the time. I see it in books and TV. I hear it in the way people talk.

All those cannibal llamas.

It makes it really hard for me to write about llamas who aren't cannibals.

James Tiptree, Jr. has a very interesting story called "The Women Men Don't See." I read it when I was twenty, and I admit I had a difficult time understanding what the fuss was all about. This was the story? But . . . this wasn't the story! We're stuck for the full narrative inside the head of a man who does very little, who's traveling with a woman and her daughter. Like the man, of course, we as readers don't "see" them. We don't realize that they are, in fact, the heroes of the story until it's over.

This was the man's story, after all. That was his narrative. It's his story we were a part of. They were just passing objects, some NPCs in his limited landscape.

We didn't see them.

When I was sixteen, I wrote an essay about why women should remain barred from combat in the U.S. military. I found it recently while going through some old papers. My argument for why women shouldn't be in combat was because war was terrible, and families were important, and with all these men dying in war, why would we want women to die, too?

That was my entire argument.

"Women shouldn't go to war because, like men do now, they would die there."

I got an A.

I often tell people that I'm the biggest self-aware misogynist I know.

I was writing a scene last night between a woman general and the man she helped put on the throne. I started writing in some romantic tension, and realized how lazy that was. There are other kinds of tension.

I made a passing reference to sexual slavery, which I had to cut. I nearly had him use a gendered slur against her. I growled at the screen. He wanted to help save her child . . . no. Her brother? Okay. She was going to betray him. Okay. He had some wives who died . . . ugh. No. Close advisors? Friends? Maybe somebody just . . . left him?

Even writing about societies where there is very little sexual violence, or no sexual violence against women, I find myself writing in the same tired tropes and motivations. "Well, this is a bad guy, and I need something traumatic to happen to this heroine, so I'll have him rape her." That was an actual thing I did in the first draft of my first book, which features a violent society where women outnumber men twenty-five to one. Because, of course, it's What You Do.

I actually watched a TV show recently that was supposedly about this traumatic experience a young girl went through, but was, in fact, simply tossed in so that the two male characters in the show could fight over it, and argue about which of them was at fault because of what happened to her. It was the most flagrant erasure of a female character and her experiences that I'd seen in some time. She's literally in the room with them while they fight about it, revealing all these character things about them while she sort of fades into the background.

We forget what the story's about. We erase women in our stories who, in our own lives, are powerful, forthright, intelligent, terrifying people. Women stab and maim and kill and lead and manage and own and run. We know that. We experience it every day. We *see* it.

But this is our narrative: two men fighting loudly in a room, and a woman snuffling in a corner.

What is "realism"? What is "truth"? People tell me that the truth is what they've experienced. But the trouble is, it's often hard to sort out what we actually experienced from what we're told we experienced, or what we *should* have experienced. We're social creatures, and fallible.

In disaster situations, the average person will ask for about four other opinions before forming their own, before taking action.[6] You can train people to respond quickly in these types of situations through vigorous training (such as in the military), but for the most part, about 70 percent of human beings like to just go along with their everyday routine. We like our narrative. It takes overwhelming evidence and—more importantly—the words of many, many, many people around us for us to take action.

You see this all the time in big cities. It's why people can get into fistfights and assault others on busy sidewalks. It's why people are killed in broad daylight, and homes are broken into even in areas with lots of foot traffic. Most people actually ignore things out of the ordinary. Or, worse, hope that someone else will take care of it.

I remember being on the train in Chicago in a car with about a dozen other people. On the other side of the car, a man suddenly fell off his seat. Just . . . toppled over into the aisle. He started convulsing. There were three people between me and him. But nobody said anything. Nobody did anything.

I stood up. "Sir?" I said, and started toward him.

And that's when everyone started to move. I called for someone at the back to push the operator alert button, to tell the train driver to call for an ambulance at the next stop. After I moved, there were suddenly three or four other people with me, coming to the man's aid.

But somebody had to move *first*.

I stood in a crowded, standing-room-only train on another day and watched a young woman standing near the door close her eyes and drop her papers and binder onto the floor. She was packed tight, surrounded by other people, and no one said anything.

Her body began to go limp. "Are you okay?!" I said loudly, leaning toward her, and then other people were looking, and she was sagging, and the buzz started, and somebody called up from the front of the car that he was a doctor, and someone gave up their seat, and people moved, moved, moved.

Somebody needs to be the person who says something is wrong. We can't pretend we don't see it. Because people have been murdered and assaulted on street corners where hundreds of people milled around, pretending everything was normal.

But pretending it was normal didn't make it so.

Somebody has to point it out. Somebody has to get folks to move.

Somebody has to *act*.

* * *

I shot my first gun at my boyfriend's house in high school: first a rifle, then a sawed-off shotgun. I have since gotten to be pretty decent with a Glock, still terrible with a rifle, and had the opportunity to shoot an AK-47, the gun of choice for revolutionary armies around the world, particularly in the '80s.

I knocked over my first two-hundred-pound punching bag with my fist when I was twenty-four.

The punch meant more. Anyone could shoot a gun. But now I knew how to hit things properly in the face. Hard.

Growing up, I learned that women fulfilled certain types of roles and did certain types of things. It wasn't that I didn't have great role models. The women in my family were hardworking matriarchs. But the stories I saw on TV and movies and even in many books said they were anomalies. They were furry, noncannibalistic llamas. So rare.

But the stories were all wrong.

I spent two years in South Africa and another decade once I returned to the States finding out about all the women who fought. Women fought in every revolutionary army, I found, and those armies were often composed of fighting forces that were 20 to 30 percent women. But when we say "revolutionary army," what do we think of? What image does it conjure? Does the force in your mind include three women and seven men? Six women and fourteen men?

Women not only made bombs and guns in WWII—they picked up guns and drove tanks and flew airplanes. The Civil War, the Revolutionary War—point me to a war and I can point to an instance where a women picked up a hat and a gun and went off to join it. And yes, Shaka Zulu employed female fighters as well. But when we say "Shaka Zulu's fighters" what image do we conjure in our minds? Do we think of these women? Or are they the ones we don't see? The ones who, if we included them in our stories, people would say weren't "realistic"?

Of course, we do talk about women who ran with Shaka Zulu. When I Google "women who fought for Shaka Zulu" I learn all about his "harem of 1200 women." And his mother, of course. And this line was very popular: "Women, cattle, and slaves." One breath.

It's easy to think women never fought, never led, when we are never seen.

What does it matter, if we tell the same old stories? If we share the same old lies? If women fight, and women lead, and women hold up half the sky, what do stories matter to the truth? We won't change the truth by writing people out of it.

Will we?

Stories tell us who we are. What we're capable of. When we go out looking for stories, we are, I think, in many ways going in search of ourselves, trying to find understanding of our lives and the people around us. Stories, and language, tell us what's important.

If women are "bitches" and "cunts" and "whores" and the people we're killing are "gooks" and "japs" and "ragheads," then they aren't really people, are they? It makes them easier to erase. Easier to kill. To disregard. To unsee.

But the moment we reimagine the world as a buzzing hive of individuals with a variety of genders and complicated sexes and unique, passionate narratives that have yet to be told—it makes them harder to ignore. They are no longer "women, cattle, and slaves" but active players in their own stories.

And ours.

Because when we choose to write stories, it's not just an individual story we're telling. It's theirs. And yours. And ours. We all exist together. It all happens here. It's muddy and complex and often tragic and terrifying. But ignoring half of it, and pretending there's only one way a woman lives or has ever lived—in relation to the men that surround her—is not a single act of erasure, but a political erasure.

Populating a world with men, with male heroes, male people, and their "women, cattle, and slaves," is a political act. You are making a conscious choice to erase *half the world*.

As storytellers, there are more interesting choices we can make.

I can tell you all day that llamas have scales. I can draw you pictures. I can rewrite history. But I am a single storyteller, and my lies don't become narrative unless you agree with me. Unless you write just like me. Unless you, too, buy my lazy narrative and perpetuate it.

You must be complicit in this erasure for it to happen. You, me, all of us.

Don't let it happen.

Don't be lazy.

The llamas will thank you.

Real human people will, too.

What Are We Fighting For?

I CONSIDERED WHETHER OR NOT THERE WERE EPILOGUES to essay collections and then went, "Eh, fuck it. There is for this one."

It's the Fourth of July and I'm on my second beer and I'm alone at a remote cabin in the Hocking Hills region of Ohio and my phone is dead, and no, this isn't the start to some horror story. The phone being dead is good because it means I can't turn on my Wi-Fi hotspot so I can't do anything but grill cheap hotdogs and drink cheap beer and burn shit in the fire pit and finish this essay collection.

Drinking and writing tends to get me to wax nostalgic, and so I am. I remember drinking home-brewed beer at a cabin in the woods in Alaska with a guy and his puppy, and the puppy kept eating its own shit. I remember standing in the cold outside my dorm in Alaska with a guy I'd been hot on all semester and him telling me, "Someday when you write all about this, I'll just be some guy you fucked," and yeah, he was right. I remember drinking White Russians in a palazzo in Florence, Italy, during a warm night while fire throwers entertained the crowd and I wondered, at sixteen, if I'd ever feel that free and content ever again in my life.

Life is a series of unrelated incidents. It is the human mind that seeks to string them together into narratives, into story. It is the human mind that gives events *meaning*. I have told you many stories in these essays, and all of them are true to the best of my recollection. But it is the meaning behind them that is left to interpretation. What events do we share? What do we leave out? Have I shown myself to be virtuous and infallible? I hope not. I am very often wrong, imperfect, difficult, anxiety-ridden. I am, just as often as anyone, a white-hot mess.

But that is just one story.

One of the things I stress to those I meet, especially young people, is that we are the heroes of our own lives, and we can be the masters of our own stories. Much of the horror of being young is feeling powerless and out of control in the face of forces that seem (and very often are) far bigger than you. One of the things you realize as you get older is that the people in control of things have no idea what they're doing, and aren't so different from you after all. It is very often inertia that keeps broken, befouled, and ridiculous systems of oppression and exploitation in place. I'm not sure if this is comforting or terrifying, but it is true.

I remember the time I sat with my work colleagues—a video producer, a print designer, and the VP of marketing—and went over our first really big marketing campaign. I was twenty-seven, and I realized in that moment that I had jumped the fence. I was one of the people making the marketing messages that people would ingest each day alongside their toast and coffee, and it was a heady and terrifying realization, because I did not feel powerful, or in control. I didn't feel like I knew what I was doing. But I was part of this system now, I was one of the message makers, and I understood the responsibility of that. I knew that we could help or harm, and I was not too confident, at the time, that we were serving a particularly just cause. But I needed the health insurance. I needed to eat. And putting my mind in service to this cause was what was going to keep me breathing.

In that moment, I wanted to do more than serve the cause of lining someone else's pockets. I wanted to have a large, loud voice that joined other voices to change the world for the better. I wanted to put my talents into the service of something far larger than myself.

I have told you already in these pages that my end goal is to "change the world." Change it into what, though? Into a better place, I'd hope. Into a place where we don't have to fight as hard to be heard. Into a place where we have not equal opportunities, but true equality that lets us all start out our lives on the same footing. I want the world to be a demonstrably better place when I leave it than it was when I came into it. Not just for me, or for people like me, but for everyone.

The truth is, though, that I don't know how to do that. All I know how to do is write (and drink, to the limit my illness allows). I know how to persevere in the face of bullshit. I know how to not be afraid. I know how to live. Sometimes living, and speaking aloud, is the most subversive act one can manage.

That, perhaps, is enough for me. But is it enough for you?

I am getting older, and though some may scoff at that (thirty-five is not old, my sixty-year-old colleagues tell me), the fact is that death and I have danced before, and though she did not win that time, each day I can hear her breathing in my ear, with every shot of medication I take and every low sugar reading I get while hiking out in the woods alone, and I am reminded that she will get me eventually, as she gets us all, because her dance card is long, and she is more persistent even than I.

I have no children, and no legacy but my work—and you.

I have the power to reach back to you long after I am dead, through these spidery marks on paper or pixels, and remind you that you have a voice, you have agency, and your voice is stronger and more powerful than you could ever imagine, and long after I am gone, you can pick up this beer beside me and carry on the work we are doing now, the work we have always been doing, the work we will always do, until the world looks the way we imagine it can be.

I am a grim optimist, and this is my hope for you: that you will be louder than me, and stronger than me, and more powerful than me, and that you will look back at me as a relic, a dinosaur, as the minor villain in your own story, the rock you pushed against in your own flight to fame, to notoriety, to revolution.

That is my wish for you.

HOCKING HILLS
SUMMER 2015

NOTES

PART I: LEVEL UP

Taking Responsibility for Writing Problematic Stories

1 "Bury Your Gays," *TV Tropes*, http://tvtropes.org/pmwiki/pmwiki.php /Main/BuryYourGays.

I'll Make the Pancakes: On Opting In—and Out—of the Writing Game

1 Christine Miserandino, "The Spoon Theory," *butyoudontlooksick.com*, http://www.butyoudontlooksick.com/articles/written-by-christine/the -spoon-theory/.

PART II: GEEK

Some Men Are More Monstrous Than Others: On True Detective's Men and Monsters

1 "Dale Cooper," *Wikipedia*, https://en.wikipedia.org/wiki/Dale_Cooper.

Die Hard, Hetaerae, and Problematic Pin-Ups: A Rant

1 "Clarion's 2014 Literary Pin-up Calendar," *The Clarion Foundation*, https://www.indiegogo.com/projects/clarion-s-2014-literary-pin-up -calendar#/story.
2 James M. Davidson, *Courtesans and Fishcakes: The Consuming Passions of Classical Athens*. University of Chicago Press, 2011.
3 Justin Landon, "Do the successful get a free pass?" *Staffer's Book Review*, http://www.staffersbookreview.com/2014/01/author-privilege-do-we -give-them-a-free-pass.html.

A Complexity of Desires: Expectations of Sex and Sexuality in Science Fiction

1 "Joan Slonczewski," *Amazon*, http://www.amazon.com/Joan -Slonczewski/e/B000APEBSM/ref=ntt_athr_dp_pel_1.

In Defense of Unlikable Women

1 "Sideways," *IMDb*, http://www.imdb.com/title/tt0375063/.
2 "Young Adult," *IMDb*, http://www.imdb.com/title/tt1625346/?ref_=fn _al_tt_1.

3 Annasue McCleave Wilson, "An Unseemly Emotion: PW Talks with Claire Messud," *Publishers Weekly*, http://www.publishersweekly.com/pw /by-topic/authors/interviews/article/56848-an-unseemly-emotion-pw -talks-with-claire-messud.html.

4 Kameron Hurley, "On Persistence, and the Long Con of Being a Successful Writer," *terribleminds.com*, http://terribleminds.com/ramble/2014/01 /22/on-persistence-and-the-long-con-of-being-a-successful-writer/.

5 Roxane Gay, "Not Here to Make Friends," *BuzzFeed Books*, http://www .buzzfeed.com/roxanegay/not-here-to-make-friends-unlikable#.nobrE0N3E.

Women and Gentlemen: On Unmasking the Sobering Reality of Hyper-Masculine Characters

1 Kameron Hurley, "Wonder Maul Doll," *Escape Pod*, http://escapepod .org/2009/07/19/ep207-wonder-maul-doll/.

2 Kameron Hurley, "The Women of Our Occupation," *Strange Horizons*, http://www.strangehorizons.com/2006/20060731/women-f.shtml.

3 Paul S. Kemp, "Why I write masculine stories," *paulskemp.com*, http://paulskemp.com/blog/why-i-write-masculine-stories/.

Gender, Family, Nookie: The Speculative Frontier

1 Barbara Ehrenreich, *Blood Rites: Origins and History of the Passions of War*. Holt Paperbacks, May 1998.

The Increasingly Poor Economics of Penning Problematic Stories

1 Kameron Hurley, "Some Men Are More Monstrous Than Others: On *True Detective*'s Men and Monsters," *kameronhurley.com*, http://www .kameronhurley.com/some-men-are-more-monstrous-than-others-on -true-detectives-men-monsters/.

2 Kameron Hurley, "One Bloke to Rule Us All: Depictions of Hegemony in *Snowpiercer* vs. *Guardians of the Galaxy*," *kameronhurley.com*, http://www.kameronhurley.com/one-bloke-to-rule-us-all-depictions-of -hegenomy-in-snowpiercer-vs-guardians-of-the-galaxy/.

Making People Care: Storytelling in Fiction vs. Marketing

1 Leo Widrich, "The Science of Storytelling: Why Telling a Story is the Most Powerful Way to Activate Our Brains," *Lifehacker*, http:// lifehacker.com/5965703/the-science-of-storytelling-why-telling-a-story -is-the-most-powerful-way-to-activate-our-brains.

Where Have All the Women Gone? Reclaiming the Future of Fiction

1   Nicola Griffith, "Books about Women Tend Not to Win Awards,"
    nicolagriffith.com, http://nicolagriffith.com/2015/05/26/books-about
    -women-tend-not-to-win-awards/.

PART III: LET'S GET PERSONAL

Becoming What You Hate

1   Laura J. Mixon, "A Report on Damage Done by One Individual
    Under Several Names," *laurajmixon.com*, http://laurajmixon.com/2014
    /11/a-report-on-damage-done-by-one-individual-under-several
    -names/.

2   Kathleen Hale, " 'Am I being catfished?' An author confronts her
    number one online critic," *The Guardian*, http://www.theguardian.com
    /books/2014/oct/18/am-i-being-catfished-an-author-confronts-her
    -number-one-online-critic.

3   Elizabeth Bear, "The following is an open letter to my friends and
    colleagues who are established members of the science fiction and
    fantasy community," *Goodreads*, https://www.goodreads.com/author
    _blog_posts/7312419-i-cannot-touch-the-rain.

Let It Go: On Responding (or Not) to Online Criticism

1   Jerry Lee, *Buzzfeed*, http://www.buzzfeed.com/jarrylee/john-
    green-responded-on-tumblr-to-accusations-of-sexual-abus#
    .huq15M01q.

2   Sam Biddle, "Justine Sacco Is Good at Her Job, and How I Came
    To Peace with Her," *Gawker*, http://gawker.com/justine-sacco-is
    -good-at-her-job-and-how-i-came-to-pea-1653022326.

3   Alison Flood, "Anne Rice signs petition to protest bullying of authors
    on Amazon," *The Guardian*, http://www.theguardian.com/books/2014
    /mar/04/anne-rice-protests-bullying-amazon-petition.

Terrorist or Revolutionary? Deciding Who Gets to Write History

1   Michael Moran, "Bin Laden Comes Home to Roost," *NBCNews.
    com*.

2   Alissa J. Rubin, "Airstrike Hits Doctors Without Borders Hospital in
    Afghanistan," *The New York Times*.

PART IV: REVOLUTION

What We Didn't See: Power, Protest, Story

1 Kameron Hurley, "What living in South Africa taught me about racism in America," *kameronhurley.com*, http://www.kameronhurley.com/what -living-in-south-africa-taught-me-about-racism-in-america/.

2 "History of slavery in California," *Wikipedia*, https://en.wikipedia.org /wiki/History_of_slavery_in_California.

3 Greg Nokes, "Black Exclusion Laws in Oregon," *The Oregon Encyclopedia*, http://oregonencyclopedia.org/articles/exclusion_laws/#.VSfNvPnF -So.

4 Elizabeth McLagan, "The Black Laws of Oregon, 1844–1857," *Black-Past.org*, http://www.blackpast.org/perspectives/black-laws-oregon -1844-1857.

5 "The Eye of the Beholder," *Wikipedia*, https://en.wikipedia.org/wiki /The_Eye_of_the_Beholder.

6 John Rudolf, "Where Mental Asylums Live On," *The New York Times*, http://www.nytimes.com/2013/11/03/opinion/sunday/where-mental -asylums-live-on.html?pagewanted=all&_r=1.

7 Tara McGinley, "List of Reasons for Admission to an Insane Asylum from the Late 1800s," *Dangerous Minds*, http://dangerous minds.net/comments/list_of_reasons_for_admission_to_an_insane _asylum.

8 "Nazi Euthanasia Program: Persecution of the Mentally & Physically Disabled," *Jewish Virtual Library*, https://www.jewishvirtuallibrary.org /jsource/Holocaust/disabled.html.

9 Kameron Hurley, " 'We Have Always Fought': Challenging the 'Women, Cattle and Slaves' Narrative," *A Dribble of Ink*, http:// aidanmoher.com/blog/featured-article/2013/05/we-have-always -fought-challenging-the-women-cattle-and-slaves-narrative-by -kameron-hurley/.

10 Parker Marie Molloy, " 'Because We Can': How Society Justifies Anti-Transgender Discrimination," *The Huffington Post*, http://www .huffingtonpost.com/parker-marie-molloy/anti-transgender -discrimination_b_4273822.html.

11 Zack Ford, "STUDY: Transgender People Experience Discrimination Trying To Use Bathrooms," *ThinkProgress*, http://thinkprogress.org /lgbt/2013/06/26/2216781/transgender-bathroom-study/.

12 Michelle A. Marzullo and Alyn J. Libman, "Hate Crimes and Violence Against LGBT People," *Human Rights Campaign*, http://www.hrc.org /resources/entry/hate-crimes-and-violence-against-lgbt-people.

13 Kameron Hurley, "A Complexity of Desires: Expectations of Sex and Sexuality in Science Fiction," *The Book Smugglers*, http:// thebooksmugglers.com/2014/01/sff-in-conversation-kameron-hurley -on-a-complexity-of-desires-expectations-of-sex-sexuality-in-science -fiction.html.

14 "Stark Racial Divisions in Reactions to Ferguson Police Shooting," *Pew Research Center*, http://www.people-press.org/2014/08/18/stark-racial -divisions-in-reactions-to-ferguson-police-shooting/.

15 Jamelle Bouie, "Why the Fires in Ferguson Won't End Soon," *Slate*, http://www.slate.com/articles/news_and_politics/politics/2014/08 /ferguson_protests_over_michael_brown_won_t_end_soon_the_black _community.html.

16 "Criminal Justice Fact Sheet," *National Association for the Advancement of Colored People*, http://www.naacp.org/pages/criminal-justice-fact-sheet.

17 "Slavery Takes Root in Colonial Virginia," *Digital History*, http://www .digitalhistory.uh.edu/disp_textbook.cfm?smtID=2&psid=3576.

What Living in South Africa Taught Me About Being White in America

1 "A Matter of Color: African Americans Face Discrimination," *Oregon State Archives*, http://arcweb.sos.state.or.us/pages/exhibits/ww2/life /minority.htm.

2 "History of African Americans in Chicago," *Wikipedia*, https://en .wikipedia.org/wiki/History_of_African_Americans_in_Chicago.

3 Aura Bogado and Voting Rights Watch, "Watch a Colorado GOP Poll Watcher Report a 'High Concentration of People of Color,'" *The Nation*, http://www.thenation.com/article/watch-colorado-gop-poll -watcher-report-high-concentration-people-color/.

It's About Ethics in Dating

1 Zachary Jason, "Game of Fear," *Boston Magazine*, http://www .bostonmagazine.com/news/article/2015/04/28/gamergate/.

2 Taylor Wofford, "Is Gamergate about Media Ethics or Harassing Women? Harassment, the Data Shows," *Newsweek*, http://www .newsweek.com/gamergate-about-media-ethics-or-harassing-women -harassment-data-show-279736.

3 Zachary Jason, "Game of Fear," *Boston Magazine* (May 2015), http://www.bostonmagazine.com/news/article/2015/04/28/gamergate/.

Hijacking the Hugo Awards

1 Jay Hathaway, "What Is Gamergate, and Why? An Explainer for Non-Geeks," *Gawker*, http://gawker.com/what-is-gamergate-and-why-an-explainer-for-non-geeks-1642909080.

2 Vox Day, "Why Women's Rights Are Wrong," *WND.com*, http://www.wnd.com/2005/08/31677/.

3 Amal El-Mohtar, "Calling for the Expulsion of Theodore Beale from SFWA," *amalelmohtar.com*, http://amalelmohtar.com/2013/06/13/calling-for-the-expulsion-of-theodore-beale-from-sfwa/.

4 Abigail Nussbaum, "The 2015 Hugo Awards: Thoughts on the Nominees," *Asking the Wrong Questions*, http://wrongquestions.blogspot.com/2015/04/the-2015-hugo-awards-thoughts-on.html.

5 Samuel R. Delany, "Racism and Science Fiction," *The New York Review of Science Fiction*, http://www.nyrsf.com/racism-and-science-fiction-.html.

6 N. K. Jemisin, "Wiscon 38 Guest of Honor Speech," *nkjemisin.com*, http://nkjemisin.com/2014/05/wiscon-38-guest-of-honor-speech/.

7 Ashley Broughton, "Minorities expected to be majority in 2050," *CNN.com*, http://www.cnn.com/2008/US/08/13/census.minorities/.

8 Jocelyn Kiley, "61% of young Republicans favor same-sex marriage," *Pew Research Center*, http://www.pewresearch.org/fact-tank/2014/03/10/61-of-young-republicans-favor-same-sex-marriage/.

9 Brianna Wu, "I'm Brianna Wu, And I'm Risking My Life Standing Up To Gamergate," *Bustle*, http://www.bustle.com/articles/63466-im-brianna-wu-and-im-risking-my-life-standing-up-to-gamergate.

10 Alex Hern, "Gamergate hits new low with attempts to send Swat teams to critics," *The Guardian*, http://www.theguardian.com/technology/2015/jan/13/gamergate-hits-new-low-with-attempts-to-send-swat-teams-to-critics.

Dear SFWA Writers: Let's Chat About Censorship and Bullying

1 E. Catherine Tobler, "Dear SFWA," *ecatherine.com*, http://ecatherine.com/dear-sfwa/.

2 Jim C. Hines, "SFWA Presidential Election Thoughts," *jimchines.com*, http://www.jimchines.com/2013/02/sfwa-presidential-election-thoughts/.

3   Anita Sarkeesian, "Anita Sarkeesian at TEDxWomen 2012," *TEDx Talks*, https://www.youtube.com/watch?v=GZAxwsg9J9Q.

With Great Power Comes Great Responsibility: On Empathy and the Power of Privilege

1   Rich Johnston, "When Jonathan Ross Was Presenting the Hugo Awards. Until He Wasn't," *Bleeding Cool*, http://www.bleedingcool.com /2014/03/01/when-jonathan-ross-was-presenting-the-hugo-awards -until-he-wasnt/.

2   Amy McNally, "The Hugos and Wossy," *Storify*, https://storify.com /infamousfiddler/the-hugos-and-wossy?awesm=sfy.co_bbl7.

3   Beverly Bambury, "How to Handle Social Media Missteps: Book Marketing without B.S. #9," *beverlybambury.com*, http://www .beverlybambury.com/2014/01/how-to-handle-social-media-missteps .html.

Rage Doesn't Exist in a Vacuum

1   Patrick Rothfuss, *Twitter*, https://twitter.com/PatrickRothfuss/status /441712235925090304.

2   Alison Flood, "Jonathan Ross withdraws from hosting Hugo SF awards after fans and writers strike back," *The Guardian*, http://www .theguardian.com/books/2014/mar/03/jonathan-ross-hugo-award-host -twitter-backlash.

3   Cora Buhlert, "The media spin machine at full power or This is totally not what happened," *corabuhlert.com*, http://corabuhlert.com/2014/03/07 /the-media-spin-machine-at-full-power-or-this-is-totally-not-what -happened/.

4   Michael Hogan, "It really is time people stopped hating Jonathan Ross," *The Telegraph*, http://www.telegraph.co.uk/men/thinking-man /10679808/It-really-is-time-people-stopped-hating-Jonathan-Ross .html.

5   Douglas O. Linder, "The Nelson Mandela (Rivonia) Trial: An Account," *University of Missouri-Kansas City (UMKC) School of Law*, http://law2.umkc.edu/faculty/projects/ftrials/mandela/mandelaaccount .html.

6   Matt Berman, "The Forgotten, Radical Martin Luther King Jr." *National Journal*, http://www.nationaljournal.com/politics/the -forgotten-radical-martin-luther-king-jr-20140120.

We Have Always Fought: Challenging the "Woman, Cattle, and Slaves"
Narrative

1 Alison Flood, "Wikipedia bumps women from 'American novelists' category," *The Guardian*, http://www.guardian.co.uk/books/2013/apr/25/wikipedia-women-american-novelists.

2 Emily Asher-Perrin, "Lady Teenage Coder Fixes Your Twitter So No One Can Spoil *Game of Thrones* For You Again," *Tor.com*, http://www.tor.com/blogs/2013/05/lady-teenage-coder-fixes-your-twitter-so-no-one-can-spoil-game-of-thrones-for-you-again.

3 Dan Vergano, "Invasion of the Viking women unearthed," *Science Fair*, http://content.usatoday.com/communities/sciencefair/post/2011/07/invasion-of-the-viking-women-unearthed/1#.VcH2S25VhBc.

4 Karen Maitland, "Sword and Scalpel," *The History Girls*, http://the-history-girls.blogspot.co.uk/2013/05/sword-and-scalpel-by-karen-maitland.html.

5 Foz Meadows, "PSA: Your Default Narrative Settings Are Not Apolitical," *Shattersnipe: Malcontent & Rainbows*, https://fozmeadows.wordpress.com/2012/12/08/psa-your-default-narrative-settings-are-not-apolitical/.

6 Esther Inglis-Arkell, "The frozen calm of normalcy bias," *io9*, http://io9.com/the-frozen-calm-of-normalcy-bias-486764924.

ACKNOWLEDGMENTS

This book of essays would not exist without the tireless persistence of my agent, Hannah Bowman. She not only championed the book to others, but also persuaded me that it was both worthwhile and possible to find a home for this collection. She gave me an outline for the initial proposal, and we hammered it out quickly, with an understanding that this was a fairly timely collection and needed to move out the door fast. She also talked me down from several Dark Teatimes of the Soul in which I'd considered nuking this project entirely. Full service agency, there.

Thank you to Marco Palmieri and Diana M. Pho for careful editing work on writing that I'd done quickly and on the fly for online audiences. There's a permanency to writing a work that's traditionally published that I don't feel when I'm writing online, and getting this collection into shape required some work.

Special thanks to everyone at Tor Books for getting on board with this book. In addition to Marco and Diana, I spoke with several senior editors and staff after the sale who expressed their wholehearted admiration and support of the book. They said that when Marco came to them for their opinion on acquiring the collection their response was, "YOU MUST BUY THIS BOOK, MARCO." I know you're not supposed to love any book more than any other, so I appreciate all of the support at the house. It's not easy to get a book from acquisition to publication day in nine months, but here we are, and I know that took a lot of hustling from a lot of people to pull off.

Irene Gallo and her crack team of artists did a phenomenal job on the cover of this collection, which came out just right. Thanks also to the copyeditor, Deanna Hoak, who had to work with my bizarre tendency to make up words and phrases that appear in no dictionary. Not to mention the fact that I have a lot of sentence fragments and comma preferences that can give even me a headache.

My assistant, Danielle Horn Beale, did the tireless work of reviewing and verifying all of this collection's endnotes, as well as pulling and formatting essays that only existed online and putting all those endnotes into the correct format. It's this sort of necessary trench work that does not get acknowledged enough in publishing. Many thanks to her for fighting the good fight.

Living out loud can have its drawbacks, and I want to thank my husband, Jayson Utz, for coming along for the ride. Many express surprise that this foul-mouthed writer has a partner, because I don't write about it. Maybe people expect that I live alone with a lot of cats (which I think would be a pretty great life, though I'll have it known that I prefer dogs). Let's just say that there are some things in my life that are so precious I want to jealously keep them to myself, and he is one of them. Thanks for having my back throughout this wild career.

Finally, though my parents are proud champions of my work, they don't read any of my fiction. I thought I'd hit a home run here with an essay collection that they may actually read, but my mom expressed trepidation on hearing I was writing stories about my life. "I'm afraid of what you've written about us!" she said. The truth is I love my parents to pieces, and though they certainly didn't teach me how to have healthy relationships with money, food, or alcohol, they instilled in me a work ethic, persistence, and integrity that have helped shape who I am today. For better or worse.

I hope this collection didn't disappoint.

THE BIG RED HOUSE
FEBRUARY, 2016